The Little

Dave Kenny is a thirty-something hack and sometimes musician who plies his trades on the mean streets of Dublin town. He also has a bright future in television behind him. Having dragged down the *Irish Press*, scuppered *The Evening News* and given the *Evening Herald* the jitters as an Assistant Editor, he is now attempting to wreck the publishing industry. He is married to the beautiful and ever-patient Gill.

Award-winning **Graeme Keyes** is editorial cartoonist with the *Evening Herald* and has been published widely including *Private Eye* and *The Guardian*. He has collaborated on a number of books and published two collections.

The Little Buke of

Dublin

(or How To Be a Real Dub)

David Kenny

**NEW
ISLAND**

THE LITTLE BUKE OF DUBLIN
First published July 2000
New Island Books
2 Brookside
Dundrum Road
Dublin 14
Ireland

2 3 4 5

British Library Cataloguing in Publication Data
A catalogue record for this book is available from the British
Library

ISBN 1 902602 27 7

Cover cartoon: Graeme Keyes
Cover design: Slick Fish Design
Typesetting: New Island Books
Printed in the UK by Cox and Wyman Ltd.

Thanks to:
Ted, for the genes
Gráinne for ironing them
and Gill for saying they still fit me.

DUBLIN. *My* Dublin.

The mere mention of her name fills the mind's nose with the intoxicating, hoppy perfume of brewing Guinness as it sashays along the Quays. And the oily bull-farts of the 7A bus as it settles down outside the old *Irish Press* building. And the eggy whang of the Liffey as the barometer raises its glass to smelly summertime.

Oh yes, the cockles, the mussels, the smoky pubs, the tripe, the onions, the Rare Ould Times, Lugs Brannigan, the boxty, the street singers, the well-fried offal, the occasional well-fried Offaly man, the coddle…

The rock stars, the writers, the whingers, the poets, the beggars, the lousers, the gougers, the uncivil servants, the pints of black stout, James Joyce, Oscar Wilde, Brendan Behan, Ha'penny bridge, Floozy in Jacuzzi, Time in Slime, Tart with Cart. Ring a ring a rosy, "Anyone for de last of de Cheeky Charlies, MISSUS?!"

That's the standard tour of Dublin for you and if that's all you want then tear out this page and throw away the rest of the book. Because The Standard Tour of Dublin is precisely what this little book is *not* all about. This slim volume is no *Biarritz* Guide Book to Dublin, no namby-pamby see-de-sights-drink-de-Guinness-and-look-for-de-craic *guide* book. It's not about famous writers and their favourite watering holes. Or brave rebels and their pigeon-poo monuments. Or food that would turn the stomach of a wart-hog. No. It's about people. Real people.

It's about Real Dublin.

It's also about *you.*

GO NATIVE

Too many people come to our capital and merely skim the surface, but you, as a purchaser of *The Little Buke of Dublin*, will learn how to immerse yourself in every facet of Real Dub life. So why not go native for the duration of your stay? When in Rome do as the Romans. When in Dublin do as the Dubs, but don't get caught. Mr Shakespeare never said a truer word and I believe that the best way to get the most out of your sojourn in the City of Traffic Lights is to become as one with its inhabitants.

Why settle for canapés when you can devour the whole feast? Why settle for a drizzle of culture when you can go skinny-dipping in it? Here you will learn how to:

- Talk like a Real Dub
- Eat like a Real Dub
- Make Love like a Real Dub
- Write like James Joyce
- Compose Real Dublin walking songs
- Become a Real Dublin Character
- Plus much, much more

So don't be a daytripper, be a *method* tourist. Get into the role. Learn how to be a Real Dub. You won't regret it, you know.

THE BATTLE TO SAVE REAL DUBLIN

In my long and not undistinguished career as an amateur anthropologist, I have studied many interesting races with vibrant cultures and colourful histories. None of these peoples, however, have been such a delight to observe in their natural environment as the inhabitants of Ireland's capital city.

These Dubliners — or Dubs as they prefer to be called — are quite unique in terms of Darwinian evolution. This is due, in no small measure, to the fact that the island of Ireland was largely ignored by the outside world until the first tourists (from England) decided to acquire some holiday homes here in the 11th century. Prior to that, neither the Romans nor the Egyptians "bothered their barney" with this remote outpost of Europe. Pliny hinted at a reason for this when he wrote to Caesar that "Hibernia [Winterland] is cold and wet, you can't get a decent café latté and the locals won't stop talking at you and offering you cups of tea." And so, legend has it that the Romans stopped their chariots at Holyhead, put up a few signposts saying 'Edge of the World' and 'World's End, Nothing More to See, Move Along There', and just pretended that Ireland didn't exist. Unsurprisingly, everyone believed them.

This long, long history of isolation and unsullied blood-lines meant that the inhabitants of our east coast (today's main point of entry to Ireland) were allowed to develop at their own pace and to their own agenda. While the rest of mankind struggled painfully along the road from knuckle-dragging troglodyte to *Homo Erectus* and on to civilisation, the tribe from the banks of the Liffey meandered down Neanderthal Lane, swung sharply into Missing Link Gardens and took the bus to Real Dub's Cul de Sac (stopping off to pick up a copy of the *Racing Post* on the way). As a result of this unhindered evolution, the Dubs are the purest breed of humanity on the planet — the most accurate rendering of Nature's great vision. And they're not afraid to admit it.

They have a language, dress code and cultural outlook that is unmirrored elsewhere on this planet. Their songs and lore are as breath-taking as their capacity for learning and imparting wisdom. Their wit is as sharp as a politician's pinstripe. Their breath has to be experienced to be believed.

On your travels through their wonderful city you will find the world-renowned, self-deprecating Dublin writers. The raucous, raspy and recklessly roguish Dub minstrels (and their musical beards). The all-knowing bar raconteurs. The whistling plumbers, the breezy bus drivers and the sporty youngsters.

Here you will find wit, wisdom, singing, dancing and general *bonhomie* unparalleled elsewhere in the civilised world — but maybe not for much longer. For this proud people are under threat and, sadly, the challenge to their very existence comes not this time from the Viking hordes or English planters, but from their own race.

The plain people of Dublin have seen their city change rapidly over the past few years. Old friends and comrades have gone. Old institutions too; the *Irish Press* (a rare breeding ground for the True-Blue

Real-Dub spirit), Eddie Reagan's, Nelson's Pillar, The Abbey Mooney, Madigan's Bar — haunts of many the old segosha[*], all gone. In their place, designer coffee houses, sushi bars, mobile phone masts, multiplex cinemas and themed restaurants have bloomed like some deadly new viral culture. This disease — a sort of Ebola of the soul — is being carried into the heart of Dublin by the so-called New Irelanders as they attempt to usurp the *real* Dubliner's rightful place at the head of Anna Livia's table. They have brought with them a pine-and-chrome coffin to bury a proud people. These 'blow-in' sons and daughters of the good times are not concerned with the spiritual welfare or inter-national reputation of Ireland's capital.

So long as they have their pop music in the pubs and their cappuccino bars on the street corners they are quite content to let the Fair City go to hell on a bicycle, with all the decency and fair play of yesteryear riding on her crossbar.

Enough is enough, we must save Real Dublin. But how? The answer to this question is beautifully simple; by recruiting more Real Dubs to swell the city's ranks. By force of numbers we can make the

---

[*] See Glossary

future 'True Blue'* for our children's children and rid the city of the soulless New Irelanders. You — yes you — can be one of those recruits.

So come with me and dance at the crossroads of a new Golden Age for the Real Dub. Together we can introduce compulsory whist drives and bingo nights. Together we can make polyester underpants a reality. Together we can watch children playing conkers and barging into the cinema for the tuppenny rush. Together we can drink slurpy pints of stout. Together we can TAKE OVER THE WORLD.*

TO SUMMARISE...

Whether you're up from the country and just want to blend in and avoid being mugged, or whether you're a Spanish student and just want to get the occasional 46A to stop for you, you'll find all you need here to mix it up and be the "heart of the rowl"* along with the best of Real Dublin.

I personally guarantee that you'll soon be a master of the gritty charm, the pithy aphorism, the

---

* Blue is the official colour of Dublin.
* See the author's *World Domination Begins at Home* (Little Bukes, £4.99).

stunning repartee that is the hallmark of the Real Dub.

Remember, it is the Real Dub's eagerness to entertain and enlighten at the drop of a flat cap that sets him apart from the citizens of the rest of the world.

That and, of course, B.O.

PUBLISHER'S NOTE

The publisher wishes to point out that the author himself is not a Real Dub. This is less to do with an accident of birth than a lifestyle choice. As the Duke of Wellington famously retorted when someone accused him of being Irish, "Just because one is born in a stable does not mean that one is a horse",[*] so too can Mr Kenny say that just because he was born outside of Real Dublin does not mean that he is ignorant of its people and their ways.

Similarly, just because you were born in Fragiliana, Rostock, Boston or Ballybofey doesn't mean that, with the proper tuition, you can't learn to be a Real Dub yourself. For his part the author has chosen to retain his anthropological brief and

---

[*] See Glossary

[*] Wellington was, in fact, an ass.

remain un-Dublinified, the better to scientifically impart his knowledge to you, the prospective student. This has not been an easy task and over the years he has struggled manfully to stop himself going native. Such are the wily charms of all things Dublin!

Section One

HISTORY, LANGUAGE
& POLITICS

WHAT IS A REAL DUB?
The Historical Perspective

Over the centuries, Dublin has spawned and spurned many famous sons. James Joyce, Oscar Wilde, Samuel Beckett and the Yeats boys are but a handful to have suckled at her ample breast, before being told to hump off and get a real job. These boys, for all their talent and — particularly in Joyce's case — love for the city of their birth, were never going to be accepted. They were not Real Dubs. So what *is* a Real Dub?

He is a citizen of the Fair City, raised hard and fast in Pimlico in the Rebel Liberties, tutored in the School of Hard Knocks and educated at the Red Brick University. He suffers fools not gladly, has an aversion to poseurs and poppinjays and is a diamond in the rough. He is a fount of knowledge, a gimlet wit and a keeper of the sacred songs of old Erin. He will stop you getting beyond yourself when your star is in the ascendant and will champion you when you are the underdog. He is not the 'arty' type.

He is a decent ould skin.

REAL DUB ANCESTRY

No one is really sure where the first proto-Dubs came from, but antiquity has left enough juicy teasers to tell us that they were a small race. The ancient gaelic song 'Molly Malone' makes reference to the 'streets broad and narrow' which indicates that parts of the original city were very cramped. Sean O'Casey's plays would bear this out.

To survive in these cramped conditions natural selection would have eventually led to the shorter inhabitants prospering in 'the narrows' and the taller more athletic Dubs moving out to the broader streets south of Hoggen Green.[*] This would have left the short Dubs at liberty to develop their own cultural identity. One early reference to a race from the shores of the Liffey, "and their short horses" can be found in the *Lebor Gabala* (the ancient Book of Invasions). Another crops up in the sixth-century tale 'The Short Horses of Da Dearga's Hostel'. Even Blessed Bosco Fogarty in his 'The Smiling Bull of Etain' posits his own theory that the Real Dub came from the Shores of Tarsus (Short

---

[*] Now called College Green — the busy area in front of Trinity. Should really be called College Grey or College Bird-Poo Colour, but green, like the bird poo, has stuck over the years.

Horses/Shore Tarsus) and yet another eighth-century tract refers to the "little men of the east, slowly dragging their short hearses ..." after the battle of Michi Marbh (Rath Eanig).

This is probably where the modern phrase 'short arses' comes from.

KNOW YOUR HISTORY

Real Dubs know everything. Every little thing, God bless them. A Real Dub will tell you that Gepetto invented the telescope, Galileo is a liqueur and Sir Walter Raleigh discovered the three-speed push bike.

And he will inevitably be right. With such wisdom endemic to the species, it would be unheard of for any Real Dub not to have the history of his race and native city seemingly at his fingertips. It is a basic prerequisite, as fundamental as a knowledge of one's own body, no less.

As a visitor here, you will only have a scant knowledge of Dublin's past, gleaned from various in-flight magazines and beer mats. With this in mind I have prepared a potted history for you to memorise. To recite it properly you must first affect the air of a man who has plenty of time on his hands. Then take a deep draught of your pint, lean back against the bar, clear your throat and suddenly thrust your head into the middle of whatever group of tourists you wish to impress, saying:

"Not everybody knows dis, but Dublin City was *actually* discovered by de Blessed Bosco Fogarty at ten past two on de afternoon of August 12th 1478 AD. He had just finished lunch. De local Vikings at that time called the place Blackpool, which in English means 'Blackpool'. De Blessed Bosco, fearing an influx of chip vans and kiss-me-quick hats, decided to change de name to Dublin, which is Irish for 'Dublin'.

De Vikings were having none of it, however, and went to war with Brian Boru and Michael Collins on Dollymount Strand de next week.

It was a messy affair and many of de city's finest links courses were rooned beyond repair, but de Dubs won the day.

De Blessed Bosco was a man of vision and within weeks he had de trams and DART up and running. Den in 1645 de Old Enemy arrived and Fogarty's followers were forced to flee to de Liberties and de North Circular Road.

It was in dese enclaves dat de Real Dub was born."

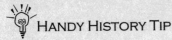 HANDY HISTORY TIP

Slip a copy of 'The Rare Ould Times' into your Walkman in case your memory lets you down.

REAL DUB LANGUAGE

As I outlined in my introduction, Dublin has a cultural identity unmirrored elsewhere on the face of the planet. While the French, Italians and Spanish may all detest each other, they are bound (grudgingly) by a common tongue — Latin.

The Fair City, however, owes no linguistic allegiances. Its own language evolved over the centuries to become possibly the most sophisticated ever to spin from man's vocal cords. If you have never heard it spoken before, you are in for a rare treat.

The first recorded use of Dublin-speak can be found buried in the historical 'Annals of Holy Aonus' (Erasmus Candidus AD 657). In a passage relating Erin's first defeat in the second Punic war with Austria, an angry Aonus refers to Cú Chulainn's[*] javelin throwers as "de greatest shower

---

[*] The Hound of Ulster, also known in Real Dub circles as Cuckoo Cullen (see Dublin characters) on account of his

of tossers[*] I seen in me life". Cú Chulainn, not being big on irony, took it as a compliment and Dublin wit was born.

LEARNING THE LINGO

The ancient language of Dublinia has a lovely, lilting, well-honed richness that the diligent student will find delightful to the ear. It is also very easy to learn. Real Dublinese (for this is what it is called) consists mainly of a complicated series of grunts, whines, click-clicks, whistles and the sound of air being sucked backwards over the teeth.

"*Click-click, ssshhhhhh* (backwards over teeth), I don't know about that missus … *sssshhhhhhh* … it looks like the head gasket is blown … *ssssssshhhhhhh* … you're looking at a fair whack of cash, *click, tut, tut, tut, sssshhhh* …"

It also operates on a system of 'reversed syllabic phrasing'. This is where the speaker never uses one

---

mad temperament. He was renowned for his prowess with the fearsome Gae Bolg, or foot spear. On this occasion Aonus was berating his men for throwing all their javelins blindly into his vanguard (wiping out half of it) on account of a bad night at the cider press.

[*] Tosser: strong-wristed individual. Perhaps Cullen took this as meaning the opposite to limp-wristed.

syllable where he can use two, or two syllables where he can use one. For instance, in Dublin the word 'spoon' is pronounced like the word 'ruin' (spoo-in). However, the word 'ruin' is pronounced like the word 'spoon' (roon).

In Dublin the word 'home' is pronounced like the word 'poem': "Wait till I get you howem …" However, the word 'poem' is pronounced like the word 'home': "Kevin will now read for us a pome about his days in the GPO …"

The word 'clown' is pronounced like the surname 'Cowen': "You're some clowen." And the name Cowen is pronounced like the word 'clown': "Dat Brian Cowen lad looks like Mick Jagger on ugly pills."[*] And so on.

THE THREE DS RULE

By far the most important thing to remember is that Dubliners can not pronounce their 'Th' sounds.

Thus 'This', 'That', 'These' and 'Those' are pronounced 'Dis', 'Dat', 'Dese' and 'Doze'. This phonetic phenomenon is known in educational circles as 'The Three Ds Rule' — or for our purposes 'De Tree Ds Roowil'. It is the cornerstone

---

[*] One of Ireland's top politicians. Seeing is believing.

of the language and is drummed into all Real Dubs from the age of three by National School elocution teachers with orange make-up, hairy upper-lips, theatrical backsides and support stockings. Invariably it goes in one ear and out the other.

The letter 'T' is also subject to some other rules. When followed by a vowel it is given a rolling Spanish R-sound. "D'ye know wharrImean?" (Do you know what I mean?), "It's a lerrer from de soshe" (It's a letter from the social welfare), "Dat's a berrer pint dan de last one" etc. However, the same letter remains unpronounced when it is preceded by a vowel and appears at the end of a sentence. Thus: "Moses took his tablahs" (tablets); "Wha?" (What?); "Did you do ih?" (it); "Van Morrison's a wrinkly old tih", and so forth.

As you progress on your Joycean odyssey through this book, the subtleties of the language should unfold before your very ears, but it would be advisable to memorise all of the above.

If, however, you're in a bit of a hurry and would prefer the quick, easy-to-navigate tour of Dublin's native tongue, then here's a little shortcut to get you through the first hour or two.

REAL DUB BOLLIXOLOGY

Every Real Dub is born with "bollix" on his lips, if you'll pardon the imagery. It is an interesting, colourful, explosive word, useful in a variety of situations. Please note, however, that unlike the 'crudite' served up by our English cousins, 'bollix' does not necessarily refer to the pudendum. Indeed, if skilfully employed it can help the average tourist cut a swathe through Dublin's social whirl. The following are a few examples:

EVERYDAY BOLLIX

The 'Hiberno-bollicks' can be used affectionately as a greeting, thus: "How's it going dare, ye bollicks?" Or as a crushing putdown, thus: "You're only a bollicks." It can be used to describe boredom, thus: "I've an awful pain in me bollicks" or to give a well-balanced critique, thus: "Dat's de greatest load of bollix I ever heard."

It can also be used to admit culpability, thus: "I made an awful bollix of dat" or to point out that an article is no longer functioning, thus: "Dat yoke's bollixed." It can also be the sucker punch in a no-holds-barred debate on some important issue of the day, thus: "Go and ask de butt end of me nut-brown bollix, ye bollix."

Compose a few variations of your own and see how well you blend in.

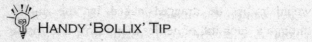 HANDY 'BOLLIX' TIP

Wear good running shoes.

REAL DUB SLAGGING

All Dubliners love to "slag" each other. Slagging is where the most disgraceful insults are traded amongst friends. It is a bonding process whereby the mettle of a pal is tested by insulting him. If the friend gets upset, it means that he can't take a joke and is not worth having as a buddy in the first place. This is a useful way of culling excess friends to make more elbow room at the bar.

The Real Dub believes himself to be the master of the devastating "slag" and prides himself on being able to insult *everybody* without causing the slightest offence, unlike Southsiders who are believed to have no sense of irony. Real Dubs say things like: "I see your mother's lowered her rates again — dare's a line of lorries down de Long Mile Road" and "Off-hand I'd say you get a lot of sex — off women I'm not so sure" to their mates, before creasing-up with laughter.

A Real Dub would never slag a tourist however. Nor would he ever tell a tourist an untruth.* He would rather be dragged naked by the ankles through a ditch full of nettles than throw a tourist a bum steer. So remember, no slagging tourists. Right?

REAL DUBS AND POLITICS

Real Dublin can best be described as a metropolitan theme park. It is a semi-fantasy world inhabited by Mickey Mouse politicians, cowboy electricians and Southside fairies. The first group of this trio is possibly the one most likely to be praised/vilified over a pint down in the pub. To be a Real Dub politician you need to be (A) a backslapper, (B) a backstabber and (C) strong-stomached enough to kiss a bingo hall full of octogenarian ould ones reeking of pee and Vaporub.

It is also helpful to have amassed large quantities of money in off-shore accounts and have a reputation for being a hard-drinking womaniser and

---

* You've just won a Ford Fiesta!

an irredeemably ruthless swine. The more money
you amass, the more laws you are perceived to have
broken and the more "totties" you are believed to
have "shagged", the greater your chances of re-
election. This is because Real Dubs love 'one of
their own'. 'One of our own' is someone who will
slip your granny the occasional fiver, have the odd
drink-driving charge quashed or arrange to cover up
that 'embarrassing' multiple murder. If Josef Stalin
or Sadaam Hussein was TD for Dublin
North/West/East/Central he would be 'one of our
own'.

The other breed of Real Dub politician is the
Angry Young Man of Dáil Eireann. This young
man (usually aged between 45 and 60) wears open
neck shirts, sandals with wine colour socks and
rides shotgun on the Glimmerman's push bike or a
Moore Street trader's pram to Leinster House. This
is to show that he is a man of the people — a
maverick — and doesn't need one of those
ministerial Mercs. He comes from an extended
family and addresses his constituents as 'brudders
and sisters'. During the week he can be seen
swilling buckets of hot sweet tea with the Molly
Malones, down at the Ilac Centre and at the
weekends he lets his hair up at Lillies or Reynards.

In times of crisis these two rival breeds of politician sometimes join forces to form 'Rainbow Coalitions'. The titles of Taoiseach, Tánaiste and Minister for Finance are changed to Jeffrey, Bungle and Zippy on these occasions.

THE VARIOUS PARTIES

It is not necessary to obtain an advanced knowledge of the political parties and the system of government. This is because all Dubliners inherit their voting preferences from their parents based on the P.R. system. P.R. being Pints Ratio, i.e. the party that buys the most, wins the most seats.

Political debate is limited to the following phrases: "How much?", "Your bank account is where?" and "The negatives are in the envelope". The following is a quick chopper-ride over the political scene:

THE MAIN PARTIES

Fianna Fáil (meaning 'Soldiers of Destiny'): The largest group in the country, renowned for putting the 'party' into politics. Perversely loved by many Real Dubs, despite having a large following in the farming community. Responsible for massive overborrowing in the early 1970s and massive hangover in the 1980s. Average follower has abnormally large amount of nasal and ear-hole hair. Says things like "Berrer de divil ye know …" and "Where were youse in 1916?"

Average TD most likely to say: "We must tighten our belts for the lean times ahead" before unbuckling his own and ravishing your sister.

Fine Gael: Not unlike Fianna Fáil, but with a tendency towards the po-faced. More popular on the Southside DART area of the city where supporters organise coffee mornings and *bric-à-brac* sales. Responsible for bringing higher mathematics into Irish politics in a bid to mop up Fianna Fáil's financial excesses. Managed to confuse everybody (including themselves) in the process. Average follower is likely to be a chartered accountant, who wears pink pinstriped shirts with white collars and cuffs and is the ultimate "square on the hypotenuse".[*]

Average TD most likely to say: "Would you like more tea, Father? That'll be 50 pence then."

---

[*] Typical example of Fine Gael joke.

Labour: Ireland's token loony left. A once-fine champion of the underdog, it now has all the political weight of an anorexic tadpole. May not know which side its politics is on, but certainly knows which side its bread is buttered on. During the early 1990s, leapt into bed with Fianna Fáil (its natural enemy), to reach the ecstatic heights of governance. The coupling, however, led to a sort of post-orgiastic impotence through the latter part of that decade after its well-endowed partner ditched it for the pretty little fillies of the Progressive Democrats.

If Fianna Fáil are the Soldiers of Destiny as their Gaelic name proclaims, then the parade ground chant of 'left, right, left, right' is not a bad way to describe Labour's recent march through political life. Average follower is likely to be a middle-class philosophy student not brave enough to join the Irish Socialist Party in case Daddy stops his petrol allowance. Also, most of the city's permanent shop stewards.

Average TD most likely to say: "We need to share out the dividends of our great success — (between the two of us)."

ECONOMIC POLICIES

Now that you know about the parties, it is important to note that Real Dub politics is concerned solely with taxes and the dole[*] — not issues. Remember, the smile on a Real Dub's face grows exponentially to the wad in his wallet.

Many Real Dubs come from the "taxes, what taxes?" school of philosophy. For example, prior to the abolition of Duty Free, if a Real Dub arrived home from Spain with seven four-litre bottles of Sangria, he would be most upset if stopped by customs. Generally he would adopt one of two stances. Scenario No 1: "How dare you, I'm an Irish citizen, have youse sumting against de Irish?" (even though it's Irish customs). Or scenario No 2, the conciliatory, philosophical, relax-the-head approach: "Customs," a real Dub would say,

---

[*] A Real Dub always takes a rolled up copy of the *Daily Mirror* with him when he's on his way to collect the scratch. This means that he can check the day's runners over a pint after leaving the dole office and not worry about being 'caught short' on the way home from the pub that evening.

"Jaysus, you can't ever have too many customs ..."
before pretending to be a Wren Boy.[*]

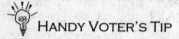 HANDY VOTER'S TIP

Talk Labour and vote Fianna Fáil.

REAL DUB FOREIGN POLICY

REAL DUBS AND SOUTHSIDERS

A whole book[*] could be devoted to the lives and
many-splendoured ways of this other major sub-
group from the fraternity of Dyflinn (that's an old
word for Dublin).

Being a Southsider is more about a state of mind
than owning a residence south of the Liffey. Cork is
south of the Liffey and nobody calls Corkmen
'Southsiders' — to their faces at any rate. However,
if one was pushed to jab a digit at a map and say
"That's where Southsiders come from", one would

---

[*] A Yuletide custom where grown men take to the streets
dressed as birds and hassle people for money. Not to be
confused with Saturday night in the Phoenix Park.

[*] Don't get any ideas, I have the copyright.

have to finger the entire south coast of Dublin as far as Bray (revolting image though that may be).

The homes of the inhabitants of this rarefied place cling to the DART line as if it was an emergency escape route in the event of the floodgates of Bogdom, Real Dublin and The Northside ever bursting open. It was for the forebears of these Southsiders that 'The Pale' was created. This was the name given to the area outside of which no tourist from England could safely step during the early centuries of the last millennium (think of a Club 18-30 holiday camp with battleaxes on). It covers, more or less, the Greater Dublin Area and its capital is a place called Dalkey.

Real Dubs consider it no surprise that the word 'Southsider' rhymes with 'Outsider'. Southsiders have never been accepted as Dubliners by those who dwell close to or north of the Liffey. A Real Dub will tell you that Southsiders are only 'blow-ins' from Wicklow and England and are not worthy of being called Real Dubs. A Southsider will tell you that they, in fact, have no desire to be called Real Dubs. They will insist that they are from South COUNTY Dublin, which means they live somewhere south of Ringsend. They call everyone who is not a Southsider, regardless of where they are from, a Northsider. Ergo Real Dubs — the

antithesis of Southsiders — are "all Northsoiders".

For many years Tara Street DART station has been the main interface between Northsiders and Southsiders — a kind of Checkpoint Charlie on the Liffey, where both parties eyeball each other across the tracks. Many's the time hostilities have broken out, with catcalls such as "Bleedin' Southsiders" and "Northsoide knackers" being hurled across the rails, while someone honks into a stairwell. The use of a mobile phone will often hasten such exchanges, drawing the inevitable "Yuppie bollix" from the northbound platform and "Drug dealer" from the opposite side of the tracks.

Southsiders are all called Nigel and Gillian and Christen their kids Mango-Banana and Penelope. Northsiders have names like Jason and Tiffany. They call their kids Jason and Tiffany.

Conservative[*] Southsiders wear Pringle sweaters, nonchalantly draped over their shoulders, Ecco deck shoes and Ralph Lauren polo shirts. Their girlfriends wear Combat pants with platform runners, Yves Saint Laurent hoodies and Calvin Klein sunglasses perched on top of their heads (especially at night). They go to rugby matches and

---

[*] The other type of Southsider is into creative body-piercing and drinks in McDonagh's of Dalkey.

drink in The Queens, The Merrion Inn, McCormack's of Mounttown and Bellamy's of Ballsbridge, imbibing minute amounts of Heineken (pronounced 'Hoynecken') and Baileys with ice before running around the bar with their knickers on their head. They also shout things like "Oid loike a point of Furstenburg with a wedge of loime, please" at the barman. When eating out they dine only in "cosy little Bistros" and meet their friends for ciabatta and double espressos after work.

RDs think all Southsiders are limp-wristed nincompoops and therefore fair game for fleecing. Bear this in mind if you choose carpentry or plumbing as your new Real Dub profession. *A meal ticket is just a DART ticket away,* as the old proverb goes.

DALKEY – CAPITAL OF THE SOUTHSIDE

Dalkey is a small ancient village, situated approximately nine miles south of Dublin City. Founded in 360 BC by Finn MacCool and Wolfe Tone, it was for twelve centuries the city's main port and boasted the finest bistros for many miles around. Unrivalled by all but the Roman Empire (if *only* the Romans knew), seafaring Dalkey carved out a sphere of influence that stretched from

Sandycove in the north to Killiney Beach in the south, carrying all things in its sway.

Following the arrival of Christianity and the Singing Brotherhood of St Gonigle in the sixth century, Dalkey enjoyed her apotheosis. Largely through trade and general interaction with other parts of medieval Erin the seafaring Gonigler Abbots built up the village's reputation as a sophisticated, worldly wise centre of Gaelic scholarship and gastronomic excellence.

Dalkey's Golden Age lasted until the late eighth century when a dark cloud slid down from the mountains and almost engulfed her. Throughout the years 780-90 the hill tribes of Glenageary, The Noggin and Bray had been swelling in size as more and more disaffected boggers moved up from the country to find a better standard of living. These furry tribesmen resented Dalkey's exclusivity and in 795 AD they waged what was to be the first onslaught of a five-year campaign to steal her marbled halls and shady arbours.

Historians agree that they would have succeeded except for the brilliance of a young general named Cornelius O'Dowda (Cornelius Longarm) at the final decisive Running Battle of Glasthule in 801 AD.[*]

The continual harrying had taken its toll, however. Weakened by centuries of late night pub-raiding by the Bearded O'Tooles of Wild Wicklow, Dalkey eventually fell to the Duchess of Saxony and her Golden Horde on St Basil's Eve 812 AD. The Duchess was not a big drinker (two glasses of dry sherry was her max) and so imposed draconian new licensing laws which placed a ban on "drink peddling" (as she called it). These penal laws meant that the town's barmen had to flee for their livelihood to the hills of Wicklow, where they continued to ply their trade out of mobile corrugated iron shacks (known as Bog Bars).

Eventually the people of Dalkey could take no more and an army was raised under the great chieftain, Garret Mór Fitzgerald in AD 918. After chasing the Duchess into the sea off Coliemore Harbour Garret rode into Dalkey at the head of a great procession, had a look around and settled his

---

[*] Cecil Hanrahan, in his excellent *Monks, Mayhem, Mad Lads* (Poulaphouca Press, 1901), pointed out the preponderance of Celtic place names that bear some reference to the male pudendum, e.g. Still-organ, Glas-thule, Lad Lane, Ballsbridge, Hackballscross. He failed to postulate any theory for this and was later arrested for asking lewd directions from an undercover Police Constable.

men on the town common, where they cracked open 304 flagons of super-dry cider to celebrate.

After four days of feasting Garret finally passed out from the drink, giving birth to his motto: "He came, he saw, he conked out". Unfortunately while he was asleep the Duchess stole back in and with the aid of the treacherous King of Leinster, Dermott MacMurrough, took the town once more.

Garret was spared, but only after he agreed to attend several AA sessions and five prayer meetings. He returned to his native Kildare a broken man and for the rest of his days introduced himself by saying: "My name's Garret, I'm an alcoholic."

Under the Saxon reign Dalkey lapsed into a sleepy solitude with her great port falling into decline on account of the lack of late pints to be had. The 'planting' of the town with 'loyal subjects' meant that Dalkey's ancient traditions and proud history were soon lost in the Celtic twilight. Detractors say that these Old Saxonians were the forbears of the modern Southsider. This may be a bit unfair, but whatever shade your politics, there is no doubting that Dalkey is undisputedly home to an inordinate amount of 'Cecils' and 'Penelopes'.

Only in the latter part of the 20th century was the town rediscovered, during the Great Houserush of the 1990s. Wave after wave of pop combos and

Hollywood starlets came to marvel at her olde worlde splendour and buy up as much property as their agents could lay their hands on. Their arrival, however, pushed prices through the roof to such an extent that the local children have been forced out of the market for a house in their home town.

The good burghers have taken it all in their stride, however, and pride themselves on their nonchalant attitude[*] to the stars and their foibles. It is not uncommon to see major Tinseltown 'names' being studiously ignored in some of Dalkey's fine hostelries. Indeed, many locals have been known to wait in the pub for hours just so they can let some rock star know he's being ignored.

If you're planning a day trip here's some info:

Best Eaterie: (Domestic) Borzas Chip Shop; (Foreign) Lee's Kitchen.

Best Place to Ignore Stars: Finnegans, The Queens.

---

[*] The Mean Streets of Dalkey, unlike Tinseltown and East LA, are not renowned for their violence, but drive-by criticisms are not unheard of (screech of brakes, "Those shoes, that handbag, I *don't* think so, *dahling!!!*", screech of burning rubber etc.).

HANDY HOW-TO-BE-A-SOUTHSIDER TIP
(Should you decide to go over to the other side):

Throw a party and greet everyone at the door wearing a silly hat, saying: "Don't mind us, we're all a bit mad in here!" Then ask them to take their shoes off "so as not to damage the pile".

REAL DUBS AND CULCHIES

Real Dubs, like their Southside neighbours, are also wary of folk from outside the Pale. They have various names for these people, such as Bogmen, Gombeens, Muck Savages, Bog Trotters, Mullahs, Muckahs, Red Necks, Culchies, Mulchies and Big Ignorant F*****s From Offaly (BIFFOs).

Lest you should think that Real Dubs' xenophobia is concerned solely with their fellow countrymen, it is important to note that they consider EVERYONE from outside Dublin a culchie. That includes Spanish Culchies, Moravian Muck Savages, Belgian Bog Trotters and German Gombeens. Not to mention Rumelian Rednecks.

According to a Real Dub, the Irish Culchie comes "up to" Dublin for three reasons. (1) To get a job as a Guard, (2) To protest outside the Dáil about the latest muck tax and (3) To do his Christmas shopping (in Clery's hat department on December 8). Mullahs who fall outside these categories come up to Dublin to become nurses (who organise dances to meet Guards) and teachers (who couldn't get into the Guards and are desperate to meet a few nurses). As a consequence of their low success rate with the caring profession, the latter spend their life rooting around in their backsides, picking their noses and 'wrapping' their thinning hair over to one side of their head because they haven't anyone to tell them not to. Inevitably, they drink too much and eventually die of piles.

Other bogmen go into the building and bar trades and say things like "Hup ye boy ye".

As a Real Dub you will be expected to be able to identify and immediately slag/ignore all men from "the country". Failure to do so is a social *faux pas* from which few have managed to recover. It can often led to the non-perpetrator being adopted by grateful culchies and having to endure interminable sheep impersonations from his former comrades. In some extreme cases pairs of velcro gloves have been received, anonymously, through the post.

 ## HANDY CULCHIE-SPOTTING TIPS

At the beach: The culchie is the one who looks like he's been taking sunbed sessions with his T-shirt on.

At the office: The culchie is the one wearing the pin-striped wellies.

At the bar: The culchie is the one arm-wrestling his girlfriend for a pint.

Still at the bar: The culchie is the big man in the blue uniform who clears the pub of late drinkers before settling in for a night "on the slate".

At the disco: The culchie is the sweaty guy with his shirt off playing an air guitar during the slow set, who leaves by himself to attend to his piles at the end of the night.

OTHER COMMON BELIEFS ABOUT CULCHIES

- They all wear hats in bed.
- Their idea of romance is a full moon and a sleeping shepherd.
- They all think Cork is the real capital of Ireland.

REAL DUBS AND TOURISTS

Real Dubs like tourists, just as they like to be liked by tourists. Their willingness to entertain at the drop of (a few bob into) a hat is legendary. So always keep your vocal cords tuned and your Riverdance kilt well-pressed for that unexpected Belgian tour party who might stray into your local some evening.

 HANDY TOURIST DANCING TIP

Be daring and wear a leather, studded man-pouch and flail those legs all over the shop. The Germans love that sort of thing, you know.

Section Two

LIFESTYLE

REAL DUBLIN FOOD

Dubliners are generally quite adventurous eaters. They are particularly fond of exotic foods from the mysterious Orient, but only after a feed of pints.

Give a Real Dub three buckets of barslops and he'll run you over to enjoy the delights of a Turkish Doner Kebab, a steamy Indian Vindaloo or a slithery Chicken Chow Mein.

However, the true staple food for generations of Real Dubs has *always* been the humble chip.

REAL DUB CHIPS

For years Outsiders and Southsiders believed that Dubliners subsisted on a diet of coddle, boxty, tripe-with-onions and slimy fry-ups (see Glossary). The truth is, however, a Real Dub would never eat such muck. Real Dubs pretend to like the above-mentioned delicacies so that they can have a good snigger as they watch some unfortunate German backpacker tucking into a plate of steaming goat's crap.

"Jaze, your norra Real Dub if you haven't earren a sheep's anus out of a broken potty, after a feed of pints," they'll say, as Gunther reaches for his wallet.

They say in Dublin that if you have half a bucket of fat, a handful of King Edwards and an Italian within half a mile you'll never go hungry. The allusion to our Mediterranean cousins stems from the Real Dub's belief that the Italians make the best chips in the world. This, when you come to think of it, is a bit strange considering they're the crowd that invented pasta. Real Dubs think pasta* is what you are when you hit 80. They eat chips, chips, chips, and more chips. Sometimes they order chips with a side order of chips.

They eat chips with fish, chips with sausage, chips with eggs and beans, chips with curry sauce, chips with egg, bean and sausage, chips with batter burgers/onion rings/spice burgers/steak and kidney pie. Steak and chips, chicken and chips, pasta and chips and of course bread, butter and chips and cheese burger and chips. Long ray with chips, smoked cod and chips, fresh cod and chips, rock salmon and chips, plaice and chips and fish fingers and chips.

---

* "Dat ould fellah's past ah" (past it).

WHERE TO EAT

All over town you'll see names like Rocca, Forte and Borza adorning the city's chip shops.

In London they have Bistro Marios, in Rome they have the Tavolo di Mercanti, in New York, Trattoria Luigi … in Dublin they have Uncle Gino's Take-Away Fish Suppers.

Real Dubs will tell you that Dublin chippers serve up the best nosh in the world. They'll tell you to "forget about all dem frogs legs and tings, who ever heard of someone nipping round de corner for a bag of snails and garlic bread?" Which is, in fact, a fair point.

Chips differ from shop to shop, absorbing the distinctive personalities of the chief chipper. Consistency is the byword for the discerning chip-eater and many hours are spent debating the merits of Mr Rocca's or Mr Forte's finest. The author's personal favourites are those which can be purchased from the Borza and Burdock families, but it's really all down to personal choice. *Beauty is in the eye of the potato,* as the man said.

I have compiled a list of some fine eateries for you to visit. Please try to remember that chips are not meant to be eaten on the premises. Real Dubs always consume these culinary delights *al fresco* and at speed (the vinegar has a tendency to melt the bottom of the bag). It is customary then for the soggy remains to be hurled back in the door at the chief chipper's head, with the cry "My compliments to the chef, good man!". This is considered a great honour, akin to the European custom of smashing one's glass in the fireplace by way of a toast.

If your chips come in a box (which is normal when being served with Southern-Fried chicken) the cry is normally directed at the chipper's wife: "Dat was a lovely bit of breast Missus, but your box was a bit greasy."

SOME EATERIES *

Borza's, 84 Middle Abbey Street, Dublin 1
(With sister shop in Dalkey, Co Dublin).

Burdock's, Christchurch, off Dame Street
(The king of the one and one).

Caffola's, 75 Mespil Road, off Baggot St, Dublin 2
(A fine establishment).

Embassy Grill, Pembroke Road, Dublin 4
(Quite upmarket, for special occasions).

Fusco's of Meath Street, Dublin 8
(Nice batter-burgers).

Fusciardi's of Marlborough Street, Dublin 1
(The cod is smokin').

Miami Café, George's Street, Dun Laoghaire, Co Dublin. (Good place to try if you're on a day trip to the Southside).

---

* Details were correct at time of going to press. These establishments favour the more modern "Dat's a grad bit of grub" compliment to the more traditional bag hurling.

Roma Grill, North Circular Road, Phibsboro, Dublin 7. (When in the North Circular Road, do as the Romans).

The above chippers are just starting points. If you take time to wander around you'll stumble upon plenty of other establishments you can declare to your mates as having "de best real chips in Dublin".

For those of you who really dislike chips and insist on eating the Darby O'Gill diet, then here is a token recipe for Dublin Coddle. Bear in mind that the resultant 'meal' should be the colour of liquidised brain and slippery in its consistency. Enjoy.

DUBLIN CODDLE

Serves 8

Coddle, apparently, means slow-cooking and you don't get much slower than this dish (or the people who eat it). It originated in the seventeenth century and can only have been brought over to Dublin by the barbarian English marauders of those tempestuous years. Usually, it is a mixture of bacon, sausages and potatoes slung into a pot of boiling milk, but for the discerning reader I have put together a slightly more sophisticated version of this delicacy.

INGREDIENTS:

1kg unsmoked bacon joint, soaked overnight
  (or a pile of rashers)

450g (1lb) sausages (Hicks are nice)

1 kg potatoes, peeled and diced

1 teaspoon thyme leaves

½ teaspoon ground white pepper

½ teaspoon of mustard powder

4 tablespoons chopped parsley

2 bay leaves

800ml (1.5pt) chicken stock

50g (2oz) butter, cut into small cubes

Preheat oven to 165C/325F/Gas 3.

Cut the bacon joint into 4cm (2in) pieces. Cut each sausage into four pieces. Combine the potatoes, onions, thyme, pepper, mustard, parsley and bay leaves. Make several layers with the rashers, sausage and potato mix in a casserole dish. Finish with a layer of potato mix and pour over enough stock to cover. Dot the surface with the butter cubes. Place the casserole over a medium heat, bring to a simmer, cover and cook in the pre-heated oven for about two hours or until the bacon is tender. Serve with doorstep-size slices of batch bread (or chips).

WHAT TO DRINK

Real Dubs drink nothing but Guinness stout, known euphemistically as 'pints'. They would never dream of touching anything else. Indeed, if it was raining champagne, a Real Dub would stay at home.[*] Ordering "a pint" entails giving the barman "a shout".

"Hey, Jem, throw us up a pint there!" is one such shout. "Barman, might I trouble you for a peach schnappes in a frosted glass?" is not. The barman, by the way, is the only person allowed to 'throw up' pints on the premises, so bear this in mind if you are tempted to have a good feed of them. Over-indulgence is fairly commonplace and can lead to horrendous "episodes" the following

---

[*] On these occasions (champagne rain is quite common in Dublin) he will drink mug after mug of tea rather than suffer "dat ould farren shite dat comes in de tins". Then when the weather clears he will leg it lickety-spit down to his local and order 14 pints just before the bar closes.

morning. These "episodes" are sometimes referred to as the releasing of a "flock of sparrows" or unsolicited "pebble-dashing". This is often put down to having had a "bad pint". Here is a typical conversation overheard the morning after a night in the pub:

RD1: "Jaze, I must have had a bad pint last night, me ring's in tatters."

RD2: "Which one?"

RD1: "I only *have* de one ring."

RD2: "No, I mean which *pint*?"

RD1: "Oh, I tink it was de sixteenth."

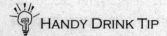 HANDY DRINK TIP

Never bring your wife to the pub. Someone might think you're gay, i.e. you prefer women to beer.

REAL DUBLIN APPAREL

Real Dubs wear man-made fabrics only, as natural fibres are not deemed manly, or durable enough. Sky-blue acrylic hipster slacks, open sandals with wine-coloured socks, snorkel-hooded anoraks and lemon polyester polo shirts (the kind dart players wear) are all runners in the Dubs fashion stakes.

Real Dubs generally wear their slacks three-quarter's way down the mast. The reason for this is three-fold: (1) It's good for ventilation, (2) It prevents chaffing and (3) Those elasticated belts with the S-shaped buckles have a tendency to 'give' with age.

The poet Edmund Spenser wrote in 1591 that "times do change and move continually". Accordingly, the relentless plod of fashion has, unfortunately, made some small inroads into Dublin's sartorial code. Younger Dubs have now taken to wearing track suits. Shiny ones with off-white socks that can be bought on Moore Street (along with 16-metre ribbons of sticking plaster) for £2.50 the bushel. This style change is largely due to Cospoir's 'Be Active Be Alive' campaign of the late '80s, where the State impugned the nation's athleticism to such an extent that a backlash became inevitable. Unfortunately, thanks to Dr Nollaig O'Neill's[*] pioneering work in cloning during that decade, 57 per cent of Dublin's under-25s look exactly the same. As a result, at weekends the Ilac Centre can sometimes resemble an Olympic village on speed.

---

[*] Dr Nollaig's greatest claim to fame was to stem the great Badger Outbreak of the 1950s. He was also the lead Zither player with 1960s' pop combo The Metaphysical Orchids.

Young Southsiders tend to be a bit more fashion-conscious than their neighbours. Like the rest of the Western youth they dress themselves according to the Marxist theory of history repeating itself. Thus every twenty years the stylish Penelopes and Noigels of Dalkey loop back in time and into their parents' wardrobes. Remember the late 1970s, when Grease was the word, Showaddywaddy and Mud slicked back their Duck's Arses and Rocky Sharp and the Replays twisted the night away? Half the female population of Killiney traded their tartan flares and Bay City Roller socks for A-line skirts and bobby sox. With a quick change of clothes the '70s had become the '50s.

Then along came the '80s and the Mod look was in. Skinny ties, button-down collars, drain-pipe trousers, pork-pie hats, Chelsea boots and parkas were to-die-for. The Who were in, The Kinks were in, Quadrophenia was in and everybody's Daddy was buying them a Lambretta for their 18th birthday. With a quick, herky-jerky groove across the dancefloor the '60s were back. Then the '90s raved in and suddenly bell-bottoms, crop-tops, platforms, Astrakhan collars, Abba, Barry White, Noel Edmonds and shirt collars the size of elephant ears were bigger than ever. The '70s had risen, ignobly, from the dead.

You as a Real Dub will not be required to chop and change in this sea of style. Always place comfort over chic and stick to the man-made fibres (literally). And to the fashion victims of the Southside say: "Marx and Spenser, how are you."

THE HOWAYAH

There is another important social type at large in Dublin. He or she is called the Howayah. The name is derived from the most common greeting utilised by this particular individual: "How are you?" which is pronounced with a silent sneer, "Howayah". Avoided by almost everybody on the island of Ireland these 'untouchables' are largely credited with having brought standards of taste crashing to the bar-room floor in many parts of the city and county of Dublin. They are also renowned for their violent tendencies after a few flagons of Blunden-Village-Super-Strong-Extra-Knacker cider.

While you will not be required to dress or act as a Howayah, it is advisable to at least be able to identify them.

THE LOOK

All Howayahs favour facial hair. However, due to some genetic quirk of fate they never manage to grow more than a slim 2" x ½" strip of fluff above their lip. This is usually encrusted with various bits of ancient kebab and other unmentionable objects.

Their hairstyles invariably fall into the following categories: mullet (short on top, long at back), crew cut (2mm long), shaved or mullet with highlights. The latter style usually turns green after exposure to daylight.

During the day these individuals favour a relaxed, casual look. Hoodies and running shoes are particularly popular as they afford the wearer both anonymity and ease of flight when caught breaking into an unattended car.

At night the hoodies are discarded for soccer jerseys which are worn with pride down the local pub. Team loyalties, obviously, may vary and sometimes heated discussions arise out of the legitimacy of some team member's off-side or offspring or whatever.

Whilst these think-ins are taking place, large amounts of cider are consumed, it being the tipple of choice, favoured over the more traditional stouts and ales of the city. The reason for the drink's popularity may well be something to do with its mobility. After all it can be consumed in various parks or trains stations with one's friends[*] without the need for the complicated taps and kegs required to pull a pint of stout.

Older Howayahs (those who remember the sartorial heights of the '80s) wear snow-washed denim jeans, with cut away slip-on shoes and greying 'white' socks. The look is normally topped

---

[*] All Howayah names end in the letter O. Some common examples are Micko, Johnno, Anto, Damo, Dermo etc.

off with a canary-yellow polo shirt with matching tie under a flecked Don Johnson Miami Vice jacket (with sleeves rolled up), all bought for under a tenner down at the markets.

Stylish accessories include 'sleeper' earrings, worn only in the left ear, because of the belief that 'steamers' wear them in the right ear to attract members of their own sex. Also, no self-respecting Howayah would be seen without at least two huge signet-rings, which can be used to end an argument over off-side decisions, dodgy penalties etc.

It is worth remembering that the average Howayah believes that being looked at is a legitimate reason to give someone a "puck in de gob". So at all times avert your eyes and don't be tempted to comment on an individual's dress sense.

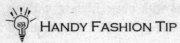 HANDY FASHION TIP

For formal occasions tuck your T-shirt into your underpants.

THE REAL DUB WALK

Affecting the proper walk is an integral part of being a Real Dub. A lot of time and effort is needed to perfect it. It can loosely be described as being a cross between the Harlem Shuffle and the Henry Street Hiproll.

To do it, affect a devil-may-care attitude and thrust forward your left shoulder. Now imagine you've got piles. Bad ones. Imagine you've got piles and you've just done the Grand National. Affect a devil-may-care attitude and alternate shoulder thrusts as you glide along. Now you have the walk.

HANDY WALKING TIP

Keep one hand in your pocket to stop your slacks from hitting the floor.

WHERE TO BUY THINGS

Real Dubs will walk a million miles for a bargain and they will talk incessantly about their purchases until you threaten violence. To blend in you must also be a skilled bargain-hunter and knowing where to go for a good deal is, obviously, half the battle.

For electrical goods such as videos and hi-fis, why not try the world-renowned Gardiner Market? This is usually held after dark in an alley off Gardiner Street and tourists are always welcome.

£25 will buy you a decent car stereo and for an extra tenner they'll throw in the car as well. Credit cards are generally accepted — though seldom returned.

For leather goods, check out the Summerhill Fair. This is particularly busy on Sunday mornings, when hundreds of hungover Dubs stumble into Summerhill (north of the Liffey) in the hope of buying back their handbags or wallets from the young men who took advantage of their inebriated state the night before. Drop along for the Lucky Dip factor. Why not buy someone else's bag? You never know what treasures/credit cards/life-saving drugs may have been overlooked by the helpful sales-person. And remember, always be prepared to haggle!

A stroll down Henry Street is a must for anyone bent on buying "de last of de wrappin' paper" or sixteen yards of sticking plaster. However, the chants and catcalls of the street-sellers mixed with the heavy drum-and-bass rhythms bouncing out of the various sporting apparel shops can be a bit disorientating for the inexperienced shopper. The sight of so many locals walking around with their hands in their back pockets may also lead you to believe that you have stumbled upon an outbreak of piles. This, however, is just a normal precaution taken by hardened shoppers too used to having to buy back their wallets down in the Summerhill Fair.

O'Connell Street is rightly famous for its aromatic herbs and spices which can be purchased every ten yards or so. Just tell the chap in the polyester track-suit to foil wrap them for freshness.

For exotic fruits, Moore Street and the George Pub on South Great George's Street measure up fully to the zouks and bazaars of the mysterious East.

REAL DUB HEALTHCARE

Real Dubs are never ill, but many die of piles. "De Johnny Giles are only bursting out of me," some say, while others announce, "I've never had a sick day in me life", before hocking and spluttering and covering you in thick black sputum.

REAL DUB SEX

Not really done. Most Real Dubs tend to shy away from such activities. Those who do indulge tend, as good Catholics, to eschew the use of contraceptive devices, preferring more natural methods. Where

* This is actually true!

the ancient Egyptians used crocodile crap and the Elizabethans used their socks, Dubliners for centuries have believed in the contraceptive power of Guinness. Unlike creams, potions, lotions or rubber devices, it is administered orally. Not before or after sex. But instead of.

If, as a lusty foreigner, you find celibacy too much to bear, then you would do well to remember the following:

- Safe sex to a Real Dub is doing it when your wife's gone down to the bingo — or when the farmer's not looking.

- Oral sex to a Real Dub is talking about it over a few pints with the lads.

Sexy Tip

Romance to a Real Dub means taking your socks off before you jump into bed.

Section Three

LEISURE

DUBLIN PUBS

Despite what Hollywood might tell you, the pub is the true stomping ground of the Real Dub — not down in Smithfield selling horses or starring as extras in Alan Parker movies. The pub is the centre of the Dublin universe and its traditions and lore should not be taken lightly. Over the centuries uprisings have been staged, masterpieces dissected, poets exiled, tramlines dug up, trophies raised and all the while Mother Pub has been on hand to serve beer and cordials and mop up after the combatants have stumbled home. Dublin's greatest names are but gobs in the sawdust, long since swept from her floor. It is Mother Pub that remains.

The following section, in its own humble way, attempts to touch upon how this proud institution affects the daily lives of Dublin's citizens. Remember, if you can blend in to a Dublin pub and not stand out like an Icelandic clog dancer at Covent Garden, then you are more than halfway to becoming a Real Dub.

THE DECOR

All genuine Dublin pubs are dark and small. The tinier and more devoid of light they are, the more the genuine article they can claim to be.[*] If they are also exceedingly smelly, then you know you're in the right place. The walls should be proudly panelled and lovingly lacquered. Over the bar should hang smoked ham shanks, bits of old bicycles, a photograph of Michael Collins, a pair of pruning shears and a 'Smoke Players Navy Cut' sign. The barman should be neatly dressed in the nattiest of aprons, his hair should be fashionably short. He should greet you with some wry comment about the weather "you brought with you" and spend the day polishing glasses and dispensing pints and sound advice in a gruff yet heart-of-gold kind of way. When you take your leave he will be genuinely sad to see you go and may offer you an ashtray or personalised match box by way of a souvenir.

The clientele should be exclusively male (including the Maureen O'Hara look-alike in the corner) and all wear flat caps and smoke non-tipped cigarettes and pipes. When you walk in they will turn their heads in unison to give you the once-over. Satisfied that you are not a peeler (a police constable), a Black and Tan, an AI man or a G man or a mobile phone salesman, they will return to the study of their pint or the reciting of their poetry.

---

[*] Think confession box.

After a while you will be called upon to sing a song of old Erin.

That is how one faithfully describes a *genuine* Dublin pub. It is NOT how one would describe a genuine REAL DUB pub.

The interior design of a Real Dub pub is generally based on two principals: comfort and modesty. In place of worn boards or cobbles, the floor should be covered in an industrial strength carpet, resistant to cigarette burns, nuclear meltdowns and/or oil spills. It should be of an indeterminate design and sticky underfoot.

The seating should consist of high chairs set around circular tables with the words 'Anto loves Jackie' and 'Fran rules A-OK' engraved upon them. The walls should be lined with settees boasting the finest stain-resistant red velour that money can buy. The curtains should be made from the same material and be sufficiently long enough to provide patches for the settees when they require repair. The bar should be either long and featureless or short and hatch-shaped with a metal grille over it.

An aversion to bits of old bicycles means that the area behind the barman is adorned mainly with A3-sized pieces of card on which are hung plastic packets of the finest American peanuts. In place of the sepia-tone photograph of a uniformed Michael

Collins there should be a photo of someone called 'Go-Go' Farrell receiving the 'Needle' Dick O'Neill Inter-Pubs Darts League Division One Perpetual Trophy. In place of the ham shank should be a sign which reads (sic):

Toasted cheese s/witches: £1.25.

Toasted Ham and cheese: £1.75

Toasted cheese and oNion : £1.35

tosted Ham cHeese and onion: £1.95.

The barman should wear a red bow-tie and a short-sleeved shirt. His pert bottom should wink roguishly out of the waistband of his black Farah sacks which are a regulation three sizes too small for him. His shoes should be machine-crafted from the finest splash-resistant nylon polymer. As a result he will give himself the occasional electric shock while pulling a pint with one hand and scratching his scrotum with the other. His name is Mick, he greets all newcomers with a friendly "Whaddya want?", and he spit-polishes the pint glasses.

Over the past number of years, Dublin has busied itself exporting Genuine Dublin Pubs to the four corners of the globe[*] in the belief that her watering holes are far superior to the bland 'café houses' of Europe, Asia and America. Now in

[*] Question: How can a globe have corners?

places as far flung as Ulan Bator or Croydon you can't walk five yards without bumping into a drunk being flung out of a Kitty O'Shea's or an Auld Dubliner. Even the Southsiders are at it, with Dan Finnegan's and the Queens of Dalkey opening up shop in Spain and Hungary respectively.

Perversely, while Dublin has been gleefully selling this jiggery-pokery to the heathen Euros, the bleak, minimalism of the Continent has been stealing into the very heart of her domain. Take one look around the quays and you will see pine and chrome 'bars' where once stood many a fine Genuine or Real Dublin pub. McCormack's on Burgh Quay is a good example of this new trend. Formerly the White Horse Inn, an ancient early house which catered for generations of rogues, touchers and *Irish Press* men, it is now frequented by people who wear 'casual chic' and have conversations with the talking clock on their mobile phones.

In the halcyon days of the Horse, the only suits allowed on the premises were spades, clubs, diamonds and hearts. Spades and clubs were frequently taken to any power-suited yuppie who strayed in off the quays.

Where once there were mean little windows behind which a citizen could hide away from prying eyes, there are now enormous sheets of glass, designed to afford the exhibitionist drinker the greatest possible audience for his purchase of a Babycham. In times past merely letting another man *look* at your pint was considered suspiciously liberal – gay, even.

Now the whole neat facade squeals 'Look at me, look at me, I'm *soooo* sophisticated' where before it promised to 'Knock de bollix off ye' if you didn't come in and part with your money. Oh, dem was de days, as its patrons were wont to say.

Whilst this transformation of the city's pubs has been taking place, many of the Real Dub establishments have fled to the suburbs to escape the fate of the White Horse. Now, dotted around the county, awaiting the day of their return, are a plethora of fine Real Dublin pubs. Due to the clandestine nature of their existence, however, it is not possible to name them here. Suffice to say that the greater Ballybrack/Dun Laoghaire/Tallaght and Killester areas might be harbouring a few of these renegade hostelries.

Baggot Street and the side-roads off Grafton Street also host one or two of the last bastions of genuineness still trading in the city centre.

REAL DUB PUB TALK

Real Dubs discuss all manner of things pertaining to the quality of their existence in pubs. They discuss politics, sex, sport, royalty ("Doesn't dat Prince Charles lad look like de FA Cup or wha'?"), more sport and how you can get two pairs of slacks, a jumper and four shirts in Michael Guineys for £4.99 (in the sale).

They DO NOT sit around in pubs with their fiddle under their oxter waiting for a tourist to wander in. They DO sit around in pubs giving out about the price of the pint and how the dole should be index-linked to drink prices and bookies' tax.

Younger Real Dubs spend most of their time bragging about their hangovers. The bigger the hangover, the better the night before. They say things like "I was so locked dey had to stick a broom handle up me hole so's I could stay upright at de bar." And: "You missed a great night, I got out of me tree, dumped in me kacks and honked me ring up in de back of de nightlink, heh, heh."

HANDY PUB TIP

Drink twelve pints and head for the Chinese takeaway. Practice your Bruce Lee impressions while waiting for your chicken balls and chips.

Examine your chicken balls thoroughly when you take them outside.

THE PINTMAN

While the fraternity of the pint is enjoyed by all true-blue Dubs, there is no bond so strong as that between the mystical Pintman and his stout.

The Pintman is a mysterious creature, believed to have superhuman powers, so named because his whole life is devoted solely to the drinking of black stout. While most Real Dubs will boast about their tolerance level and the number of pints they are capable of skulling, they still manage to find time to take on a little work or go to the toilet occasionally. The Pintman, however, will always stand his ground at the bar and never succumb to the corporal pleasures of food, job, wife or bed. He just drinks. And drinks and drinks and drinks. Occasionally he might stop in mid-swallow to dispense some piece of advice, but in the main he just stares at his pint, nurses it a little, then glugs it back to make way for the next one. He then carries on drinking. And drinking. And drinking.

It is as much for his extraordinary capacity for fluid intake as it is for his enigmatic presence that he is revered and (slightly) feared by his pub fellows.

A Pintman is normally no more than five-and-a-half-feet tall, although he seldom reaches his full height so stooped is he with the bulbous Zeppelin hanging over his waistband (the bigger the belly, the better the Pintman). He often wears his cap indoors and seldom appears to go to the toilet. No one is sure from whence he came or whither he goest after an evening down the pub. He is a set fixture in most establishments, like a toilet-roll dispenser, and is invariably named 'Old Joe' or 'Paddy the Pint'. His conversation is generally limited to a knowing nod at the barman when his pint is two-thirds empty or the word "pint" when the bar is crowded. Often his stout will magically appear before him and vanish just as mysteriously. He will *always* get served before you, such a valued customer is he.

The house Pintman is always the last to leave the premises and always the first to return in the morning.

Some don't leave at all. Indeed, that most famous of all Pintmen, The Toenail O'Rahilly, lived for 67 years in the Abbey Mooney pub before the barmen discovered he had a wife and seven children living a short distance away on Gardiner Street.

This led to a tightening of the laws on hospitality around Dublin's alehouses. Now the barman will shout "Have yez no homes to go to?" at the end of a night's drinking and you will be expected to say yay or nay depending on your domestic arrangements. Should you indicate that you do not have a home to go, you can be sure of a friendly ear, a camp bed and buckets full of late stout.[*]

The imbibing skills of the Pintman are always a topic for heated debate. Real Pintmen are believed to consume at least 30-40 gallons of Uncle Arthur's milk per week. Only the barman knows how many pints an individual has lowered on a given night, and while this can be reckoned in the 20-plus bracket, a Pintman almost never gets drunk.[*] He also never sits down or falls over.

It is considered unmanly and disrespectful to drink or receive a pint whilst seated or face-down on the floor. No matter how mouldy or 'gee-eyed' the pintman becomes he will still manage to anchor

---

[*] Try it, it works.

[*] Real Dub drinkers never ever get drunk. They get stewed, tipsy, plastered, blotto, stocious, paralytic, jarred, mowldy, well-oiled, maggoty, well-on, fluthered, pickled, drunk-as-a-skunk, under-the-weather, creased, three sheets to the wind, twisted, locked or rat-arsed.

The word drunk on its own is not considered to be flexible enough to describe the level of inebriation attained by the imbiber. For example one may get slightly tipsy or a little muzzy after five pints while ten pints will make you well-on. Fifteen pints will get you fluthered while twenty will get you stocious and so on.

himself to the bar. Cynics might put this down to a certain painful disorder in the trousers, brought on by too many treacly pints and undersized Y-fronts. Others, however, say this fastidious adherence to the rules of drink etiquette has its roots in a dim-and-distant Celtic ritual ...

THE LEGEND OF STOUT-HEARTED GOBNAIT

The Rite of the Pint makes its first literary appearance in the fifth-century tale, *The Wooing of Stout-Hearted Gobnait* (National Library of Ireland). In this story a fair princess, Gobnait of the Freckled Pig, must prove she is worthy of the men of Leinster (known then as Leighin). To do this she must be able to run like the clappers through a field of gorse bushes without tearing her frock, duck beneath a stick held two inches off the ground, leap sixty yards into the air, somersault, catch a ball of twine between her buttocks, knit two *geansai* (sweaters) before her feet touch the ground, be buried up to her oxters in badger poo, strangle twenty-four slavering bull mastiffs and pull the perfect pint.

She accomplishes all the tasks placed before her but finds the latter the most difficult of all. For as the scribe, Scottus Fluthernicus, wrote: "A pint, according to the traditions of that time, must be coaxed out of the tap, like unto the maid drawing milk out of a goat's tit. It is squeezed, yanked, pulled, teased and cajoled into the grateful cup. It is then left to stand until it has attained the colour of lacquered ebony, topped-off and placed with ceremony before the imbiber, for it is never placed in the hand. The puller then utters the benediction "Make a hole in dat" and the pint is scrutinised, caressed and lowered down the drinker's neck. The fire of thirst quenched, he will then reply: "Dat hit de spot."

Fluthernicus goes on to say that for either party to be seated during this ritual would be as blasphemous as "peeing in St Kevin's Bed", such was the respect then afforded to the "consecration of the pint". Happily for Gobnait, she managed to perform all the above, find herself a husband and live to a ripe old age, until she fell out of a chariot.

REAL DUB REMINISCING

Dublin pubs are always brimful of 'old segoshas' and their "fond memories". Real Dubs don't generally need any stimulus to reminisce, but the swish of a barman's apron is guaranteed to send them peddling furiously down memory lane.

Misty-eyed Real Dubs say things like, "Ah tings was berrer in de old days, son. You could take a mot out to de pictures, treat her to two pints of plain, 20 Woodbine and a one-and-one in Burdocks and still have change out of a penny after paying her tramfare home. Dem was de days Godblessusand-saveus. Amen."

They also knew all the characters, "Janey, I'll never forget de night meself and James Joyce met Brendan Behan, Bang Bang, Fortycoats, Archbishop McQuaid and Matt Talbot in de back room of de Mucky Duck ..."

Sometimes they like to talk about their childhood: "Did I ever tell youse about de day me and de lads went fishing for pinkeens in de canal before sunrise, boxed de fox after breakfast, took a dip in de Forty-Foot, learned our Gaelic pomes in de hedge school down at Beggar's Bush, went to High Mass, played Marbles, Ring-A-Ring-A-Rosy and Blind Man's Bluff before dinner, climbed Nelson's Pillar and fought shoulder-to-shoulder with Padraig Pearse before de mammy called us in for tea?"

REAL DUB CHARACTERS

As witnessed above, the celebration of Dublin characters[*] is a favourite past time of the Real Dub. They take their nose out of their pint when there's a lull in the conversation, look wistfully into the half-distance and say: "Ju know wha'? Dere's no carcters anny more."

They then proceed in the best Homeric tradition to litanise all the characters of yore.

"Ju remember Bang Bang, his da was from de Long Mile Road, what a bleeding header, and Ziggy Heil, he was some looper — used to think his push-bike was a tank and Holy Mary, mad ould one nearly kilt me wid her cross, got it specially made out of giant Japanese Bonzo trees so she could box de heads off de young ones coorting up in de bushes off Stephen's Green ..." and so on.

---

[*] To be a Dublin character you need to be able to stink to high heaven, cadge pints, curse in at least one language, throw a punch without ever connecting or spilling your drink, worry horses, wear chains, claim to be a poet/writer/painter, play an invisible kettle-drum while farting the National Anthem and/or make a thundering great nuisance out of yourself.

Dublin characters all had strange names, like the Glimmerman, Forty Coats,[*] Matt Talbot (named after a bridge), Zozimus, Fluther Good and the Bird Flanagan. This comes from the Dubliner's special talent for making up nicknames. Two weeks after the Anna Livia fountain was unveiled on O'Connell Street, some wag had christened it the Floozy in the Jacuzzi; the same went for the statue of Molly Malone on College Green — it was renamed The Tart with the Cart because of her outsized 'mussels'. Ditto all Dublin characters.

For instance, if your name was Seamus Kelly and you were a well-known but eccentric mechanic, your nickname would inevitably be The Shayk (shay kelly + oil = sheik = Shayk). Similarly, if you walked into a Dublin Pub and said your name was Chris de Burgh you'd probably walk out with the moniker Christy Burke.

'DAT VERY SPOT'

Whilst reminiscing about Dublin's characters you must also be able to regale tourists and Southsiders with a history of the 'very spot you're standing on'.

---

[*] Forty Coats' real name was Nigel Forte Coates. He came from a very old Dublin family. They were all over seventy.

"Dat's de very bush where Brendan Behan pooed in his pants after Holy Mary tried to clatter him with her cross" ... or "Dis is where Forty Coats used to get his laundry done" ... or "Dat's where I taught Luke Kelly to play the Armenian nose flute" etc.

Geography does not play a major part in this. A Real Dub should be able to stand in the Centre Court at Wimbledon or atop the Lincoln Memorial and still manage to tell you how Zozimus bought some dodgy mussels off Molly Malone "on dat very spot".

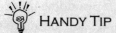 HANDY TIP

Become a Real Dub character. Just choose a name from one of the following, and away you go: The Moxer Lonergan, Pony O'Toole, Fatso Doyle, Lugs Mulqueen, Francie 'The Bike' Cauldwell, Skanky Bellhop, Sixtychins, Mother O'Jayzus McGuire, Skreeder Ryan, Jimmy 'The Jam' Butler, Rashers O'Boyle, 'Arty' Fagan, Lazarus, The Bishop Wheeler, Brush O'Hehir or Samurai McManus.

REAL DUB SPORT

Real Dubs love their sport. They will tell you that they love racing, soccer, GAA (pronounced GAH), hurling, greyhounds, snooker, pitch-and-putt, croquet, pitch-and-toss and kick the can.

"I was de 1947 wurreld champeen at kick de can," they will boast, and quite possibly they were. They do not love sports like rugby, sailing, archery, show-jumping and Formula One. These pursuits are all beloved of Southsiders and as such are "girlie sports". Although the purpose of this book is to teach you how to be a Real Dub, it is advisable not to repeat the latter phrase to the forward line-up of Lansdowne Rugby club. Certainly do not make obvious cracks about hookers.

GAELIC GAMES

Martin Luther King may have "been to the mountain" but all true-blue Dubs have been to The Hill. There is no pastime more beloved by the Real Dub than spending the afternoon down in Croke Park watching the GAH. Here he can roar his encouragement as Dub and Bog sportsmen man-fully kick their balls around the pitch. (This usually begins well before the match and ends when the referee calls both sides in for the Angelus and a cup of tea "in their hand" seventy minutes later). There is, however, one place and one place alone from where the Real Dub will observe these activities, and it is called The Hill.

The Hill — or Hill 16 — is a vantage point constructed on the mangled remains of chariots and siege weapons discovered in 1936 at Portobello Bridge and believed to be genuine artefacts from the historical Battle of Charlemont Street in 1716. It is venerated by all true-blue Dubs as a mystical place. Legend has it that Finn MacCool's hairy warriors of Old Dublin still do battle there with the ghosts of the Black and Tans in the wee hours "when there's no one about to hear or see them …". There is plenty of evidence to suggest that this is actually true as no one *has* ever seen or heard them. On the other hand this may be just an old story to keep the culchies away. However, no one has ever found one muckah brave enough to go there at night to check it out. [*]

But I digress. Every summer it is *de rigeur* for a Real Dub to visit Croke Park for the Annual All-Ireland Championships. The championships are

---

[*] His name was PJ MacMuckface and search parties are still combing the place for him.

contested by all able-bodied men from the isle of Erin and include many different competitions. One of this narrator's favourites is the skimpy shorts competition, where players compete to see who can run around wearing their tightest pants without tripping over their lunch box. Then there's the who-can-roll-their-socks-down-the-most competition, which goes way back to the dark days of the ban on shin-pads. These games, along with Gaelic Football and Hurling,[*] attract Bogmen and Real Dubs in their hundreds of thousands to Croker each year, which causes a few problems with the parking.

SOCCER

Real Dubs also love National League Soccer. They support teams called Bohemians ("Go on de Bohas"), Shelbourne ("Super Shels, come on de Super Shels") and Shamrock Rovers ("We are, we are, we are de Mujahadin. Super Dooper Super Hoops!"). They say things like "Gowan ye good ting" to encourage their players, and "Watch your house" when their defence is threatened.

---

[*] Americans please note: this is not a competition between compulsive overeaters. That game is called 'darts'.

Southsiders say "Boot it up the pork, Noigel" and "Droive* it lads".

Soccer fanaticism reached its apotheosis during the World Cup campaign of Italia '90. For weeks the city was agog as Republic of Ireland manager Jack Charlton led a merry band of men into the quarter-finals of the world's greatest tournament. Every pub from Northside to Southside was bedecked in green, white and orange, bodhráns thumped out of every door, brides got married in their Ireland jerseys and the chant of Óle Óle Óle turned the city into one enormous bull ring.

Unfortunately, as the '90s progressed and the results became increasingly poorer, interest died away. Still, the memory of Jack's Army* remains.

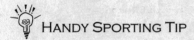 HANDY SPORTING TIP

Sit in a bar and tell tourists that you're a big sportsman yourself. Then point to the telly, cough consumptively and say: "I do love de soccer and de racing."

---

* Drive. As in "push the ball past those chaps".

* The fans were so named because of the huge numbers of them charging to the toilets (see Glossary) at half-time.

TELEDUBBIES.

Section Four

CULTURE

WARRIOR POETS

Real Dubs pride themselves on being the most cultured people on the face of the planet. Nowhere else on earth can you find so many famous writers, poets and musicians all vying for space at the bar. This great tradition can be traced back centuries to the great days of the warrior poets.

The impact of these heroes on Real Dublin history can not be underestimated. In every major battle, from the arrival of the Vikings to the glorious War of Independence, the presence of a writer in the trenches proved central to the fortunes of the Real Dub forces. Take, by way of an example, the glorious 1916 Rising (in which this writer's grand aunt played a significant role)[*]. When the English Fifth Army received a message on Easter Monday morning that the "men of letters have taken over the GPO", they despatched a tender of squaddies under a Major H.F. Burginton Winthrop-Smyth to break up what they foolishly thought was a sit-in by disgruntled postmen.

According to one eyewitness the unfortunate Major got as far as: "Back to work Paddy, those letters had better be …" before being forced to run

---

[*] This is actually true.

for cover.[*] The subsequent confusion gave the Real
Dubs a good head-start in the ensuing scrap and the
place of the belligerent writer was assured in Irish
military lore. In the following section you too will
learn how to become a respected Real Dub
author/minstrel/poet.

There will be no need for gunplay, however.

REAL DUB WRITERS

To be a Real Dublin writer it is not necessary ever
to have written a line or had anything published.
None of the Dublin writers who frequent the city's
literary pubs would, under any circumstances, "sell
out" to a publisher. They will tell you that only
"pornographers, romance novelists and biograph-
ers" do that. And "grubby little tour-guide pedd-
lers", should you mention this author's name.

The sign 'Work in Progress' can be seen
adorning the walls of many of Dublin's snugs as the
Fair City's writers wrestle with syntax and a pint
glass, while discussing the Great Irish Novel they
are working on. This novel will never see the light

---

[*] Taken from *Guerrillas in Our Midst: A History of Irish Warfare*
by Stiofán Óg MacBollogeen.

of day, because every Tuesday in a shrieking fit of creative rage, they rip up the four pages they wrote the previous week and head home to their mother's for "a rest".

Most of these writers harbour dreams of being found dead, semi-naked with a bottle of *Crème de Cacao* in one hand, a copy of *La Mouche* in the other and a coked-out gerbil asleep on the pillow beside them. In these dreams their unfinished manuscript is always discovered tucked into a pair of rancid underpants, published to great acclaim and goes on to win the Booker prize.

In reality, to be a Dublin writer (unpublished) you first need to find a 'grotty little bedsit'. Then you need to block up the bath and windows and stay indoors for two weeks living on Easi Singles, corn flakes and chocolate raisins. Then when you are starting to smell like a kipper that's been left in a sock under a radiator since Christmas, unleash yourself on the nearest pub carrying a wodge of dog-eared and stained foolscap.

On arrival, find the person least interested in talking to you, bum a pint and insist on having a conversation. Bring the subject around to literature, disagree with everything they say and challenge them to a fight. They will of course decline because you are, now fully revealed to their eyes, A Dublin Writer.

FIGHTING THE SYSTEM

All Real Dublin authors, published and unpublished, have enemies, real and perceived. This is because it is the *raison d'être* of every RD-writer to be at odds with the world, challenging begrudgery and sham artistry wherever he may find it.

"A man without enemies is a man who has not kindled the fire of emotion in the breast of his fellow man." Thus spoke Zozimus.[*] And the point is well-made. After all, a man constantly on the battlements of life is a damn sight more interesting than a man dozing on a settee. Take the poet Patrick Kavanagh. He had the formidable Brendan Behan to contend with. One can only now guess at the sparkling *badinage* and intellectual haymakers traded by these two giants of the 1950s' literary pub crawl.[*] Both are now revered as well-greaved and godlike.

---

[*] Perversely, this Dublin 'character' had more friends than you could shake a stick at. Which he frequently did, if James Joyce was to be believed.

[*] "You're only a dozy old Monaghan bollix" and "Feck off ye jackeen wankpot" spring to mind.

Today the highly talented Roderick Doyle has managed to find fame and fortune despite (or as a result of) several running battles with the nose-thumbing Establishment.

If you are seriously bent on becoming a Real Dublin writer then it's important to make an enemy as soon as you can, or nobody will take you seriously. If some begrudger is not thwarting or tormenting you in your literary endeavours, then you have no excuse for failing to deliver your Magnum Opus to the World. In other words, you run the risk of being found out. One or two strategically dropped references to livestock/rough men from around the docks/plagiarism should be enough to create the foe of your choice. Keeping him can often lead to long, hard sessions in the pub and may involve attending the occasional First Night with the contents of a market gardener's skip under your arm, but it is altogether worth it in the long run. The next module contains the best-known method for making your enmity last.

FOEBAITING

Once you have made a foe you must be able to bait him and confound him in a social setting. The method favoured by most Real Dub writers is somewhat akin to the comparing of willy sizes behind the bike shed, but not quite as sophisticated. We will call it the 'my literary circle is bigger than yours' technique, for now. This is where one author tries to out-do the other in literary name-dropping.

"Oh, Jonathan Swift was a quare man for de quick snoot of gargle," one will say. "Many's de time we used to take a slippier* out of St Pat's before evening Mass and head down to de White Horse for a pint and a ball of malt. And dat's where de phrase 'I'm going down de pub for a Swift one' comes from."

The purveyor of this little-known fact will then slam his pint down on the counter, wipe the froth from his moustache and glare at his adversary. Of course his foe will rise to the bait and soon the air will be filled with the names of famous writers they have known and gone on various skites with. You will get the hang of this very quickly, but to give you a headstart, here are a few names for you to weave a good yarn around:

Oliver Goldsmith, James Joyce, Samuel Beckett, Oscar Wilde, Oliver St John Gogarty, Lennox Robinson, Sean O'Casey, WB Yeats, Roddy Doyle,

---

* See Glossary

Brindsley Sheridan, Cedric Mulligan and/or Flann O'Brien.

WRITE LIKE JAMES JOYCE

Dublin writers are renowned world-wide for their *innovativeness* and *versatility*. James Joyce, Samuel Beckett, WB Yeats, Flann O'Brien (although a blow-in) were all brilliant *innovators* in their chosen spheres. Sean O'Casey, on the other hand, could turn a lovely wooden salad bowl for you in the morning before banging out a bit of a play before sunset, such was the *versatility* of the man.

Also — and not many people know this — Brendan Behan became a dab-hand at crochet in his youth, owing to some confusion over mallets and hoops, while Oliver St John Gogarty was a part-time barman on Nassau Street. All that being said, it is not too difficult to learn how to innovate and be versatile. You too can write like James Joyce, if you follow a few simple rules:

1) Never use punctuation oh no
2) Never mind the quality feel the length (*Ulysses* is pretty damn long, Missus)
3) Never be afraid to be crude
4) Never make sense

So now, we must find a topic to write about. For the sake of brevity we will choose getting off the Number 30 bus to buy some chips in Zorba's of Blanchardstown.

There should be an element of dramatic tension in this, so we will imbue our hero with the quality of indecisiveness as he struggles with ineluctable modality and what to have for his tea. Thus:

THE LOTUS EATERS
(After *Ulysses*, a novel by Mr James Joyce)

Bull-fart of sighing. Not this stop the omnibus settles down exhaling deeply.

Shhhhhhh.

Omnibus. Omnibus. Deus Omnibus vobiscum leder hosen terminus.

"Gerrup ourra dat we're at de terminus."

The voice subsides. Parting of clouds, straightening of lashes, struggling through parted doors Francie alights and walks crookedly to Zorbas.

And let our crooked chips, amen.

"Next?" Stately plump Angelino, in rolled up sleeves, wipes a droplet of sweat from his brow, leaving a snail-trail of oil across his forehead.

Smoked cod and a large single large of largeness and larger still.

No, heart change.

Bunburger and a single yes a pat of burger dewy beads of juicy juiciness rain down beneath a canopy of sodden cheese and break on bed of snot green lettuce leaf. Those buns so tight yes

"D'you want salt and vinegar wid your chips?"

No.

No, wait.

Wait yes. Yes!
Yes
Yes
I will
Wait Yes!
Oh Yes!!!
I WILL!!!!

REAL DUB MUSIC

"Ladees and gendelmen … May I introjuice Mr Banjo McGonigle and de Lampy Jugs, with dare own rendition of de old Dubbellin classic, 'The Stroppy Kipper'."

Real Dubs love their music. "Ah you can't bate an ould sing-song," they say. Real Dubs sing and whistle all the time, even, as the legend would have us believe, in their sleep! All the best whistlers go into the plumbers' union at a young age while all the best singers become bus drivers, where it is mandatory to know by heart the words to 'Delilah'. Generally the songs they sing can be divided into the following three categories:

EASY-LISTENING

This first category consists mainly of Tom Jones and Engelbert Humperdinck numbers with the occasional bit of a Perry Como (at Christmas) and a 'Frankie' thrun in for good measure. These songs are sung by bus drivers, butchers, carpenters and electricians (chippies and sparks) at weddings, work and outings to the pub with the missus and her sisters. Generally they are performed in a sweaty red-faced lather with eyes shut and arse and belly thrust out in perfect counterpoint to each other. The experienced performer will punctuate his number with circular movements of the left hand similar to that of a person washing windows. Or a pervert fondling a breast.

REBEL SONGS

The above category is a shady one. Songs have titles like 'Hand me down my rifle my blind, white-haired, crippled, widowed, deaf Grandmother, I have a man's work to do'. These are, *intriguingly*, whistled by foreign medical interns as they do rectal examinations for piles.*

---

* Some of you are saying 'I don't get that'. That's why it's *'intriguing'*.

REAL OULD DUBLIN SONGS

This third category is by far the most interesting. Most Ould Dub songs refer to things like prostitution ('Take her up to Monto'), drugs ('An uneasy feeling came o'er me stealing'), traffic ('The Rocky Road to Dublin') and walking.

Three-thousand-two-hundred-and-seventy-five Dublin songs are about walking. James Joyce once boasted that if Dublin were burnt to the ground it could rebuilt by using his books as a blueprint. The same applies to Dublin walking songs. They are the greatest geographical record of the city in existence and as such are revered by scholar, musician and town-planner alike.

Dublin walking songs all start off with the words 'As I roved out', 'As I went down' or 'As I was going over'. Some begin with the exhortation to take the singer to some specified destination for some unspecified purpose. Take her up to Monto[*], being one such example. Others boast about how long the singer has been walking around for ("I've been a wild rover for many's the year …"). They all, however, proceed to meander through the city's streets taking in the sights, like Nelson's Pillar, The

---

[*] A notorious red-light district referred to in *Ulysses*.

Metropole, Synge Street School, Biddy Mulligan's House, Burdocks and The Civic Offices.

These are wistful and nostalgic songs, recalling days of yore when you could leave your door open day and night. The days before video recorders and other easily transported electrical goods, if you will. As a student of Dublinia you could be called upon at any time to recite the names of all the city's monuments and characters, past and present. What better way to memorise them than in a rhyme set to some haunting melody, such as; "The Pillar and the Met/the Regal and the Press/Fortycoats (what a loony!)/Who'd forget The Abbey Mooney?"

Most of the classic walking songs of old Dublin were written under the watchful ear of perfidious Albion and the Black and Tans. Due to their cartographical nature they were a favourite vehicle of the warrior minstrels in their battle to free Erin from the talons of tyranny. Because of the millions of different locations mentioned in Dublin's walking songs, a freedom fighter could stand on a street corner and sing his orders to his men as the redcoats looked on, none the wiser. This was a favourite stunt of the bold Michael Collins during the 1872 campaign against the Prussian Junkers, which he later used to devastating effect in our War of Independence.

Mick, as he was known to the boys, loved nothing better than to stand at the top of Grafton Street in his old, tattered coat with his finger in his ear, wailing a customised version of 'Raglan Road' at his men as The Ould Enemy strolled by, with their bearskin hats and umbrellas. "On Raglan Road," he would sing, "in Number Se-ven-teeee, there's a Tan who-oo needs to be plugged ..." and so on.

As a tribute to Mick's genius and considerable influence on Irish history, most of his walking songs have not yet been decommissioned. Because of their hidden meanings and the role they played in the building of our nation, many scholars place them on a par with the revered *Aisling Gheall* or vision song, much favoured by the bog poets of the late 1950s.

After The War of Independence, the themes of most walking songs turned from the use of arms to more mundane matters, such as sex and drugs and gratuitous ambling. Still, as long as Mick's boys were writing them, the tradition of the hidden message continued to be the norm.

During the late 1960s a revival in Irish folk music meant that many of these songs came to be recorded for the first time. The old guard of Mick's Brigade had all died away by this stage and with them had passed the secret knowledge used to prise the real meaning from the lyrics. A complicated system of decoding was therefore needed to get to the message between the lines.

The most widely used system of deciphering was devised by Banjo McGonigle. His own classic 'The Stroppy Kipper' (recorded in Dublin in 1968 with his band The Lampy Jugs) is considered by many to be Dublin's finest example of 'folk duplicity'. There isn't sufficient room here to outline the exact details of The Banjo Method, but suffice to say that it revolves around a series of code words and "mewsical nooances" discovered by Banjo.

The fact that Banjo was a very large man, prone to mood swings (he once got into a fight with a marauding band of mercenary nuns), meant his method became the industry standard in a very short time[*].

A middling to good example of Folk Duplicity in a Dublin walking song can be found in 'The Spanish Lady' (Whack fol the tooral looral laddy).

It was written about a Spanish Student who had missed her 46A bus home after stopping to get a bag of chips. She is foolishly waiting for another to arrive. The narrator is doing what all Dublin songwriters do — wandering around the capital,

---

[*] See the Banjo 'Puck in the Gob' method.

continuously getting lost and ending up back at the bus-stop. What the writer's intended destination was is anybody's guess, but it is apparent to even the most superficial scrutiny that he has a lousy sense of direction.

The first verse goes:

1) As I went down through Dublin city, at the hour of twelve at night,

2) who should I spy but a Spanish lady washing her feet by candlelight.

3) First she washed them, then she dried them

4) over a fire of amber coal,

5) in all my life I ne'er did see such a maid so sweet about the soul,

6) with your whack fol de tooral looral laddy

7) whack fol de tooral looral lay,

8) whack fol de tooral looral laddy,

9) whack fol de tooral looral lay.

Using the Banjo Method this translates as follows:

1) As I got lost in Dublin city and was worried about getting mugged.

2) who should I see but a Spanish student standing at the 46A bus stop with a bag of fish and chips.

3) First she ate a chip and then she ate some fish,

4) washed down with a can of Diet Coke.

5) In all my life I've never seen anyone eat a bag of chips and a piece of fresh plaice so fast.

6) The chorus is a solicitation so charged with sexual innuendo that the publisher's Legal and Morality Department insist that it must not be printed. The words whack, laddy and lay will give you some indication of the reasons for this.

The song continues in much the same vein for thirty-seven verses, with a few word changes until the singer finally stops harassing the girl and shags off home for his breakfast.

HANDY TOURIST TIP

Write your own walking song. Merely substitute your own home town for Dublin, e.g. 'As I went down through Bremerhaven/Washington/ Nagasaki/Borrisoleigh' etc. and impress your friends back home.

OTHER RECOMMENDED LISTENING:

The Wool Tones: *Fightin' Talk* (Parlourphone).

Jamsy Fagan and the Liffey Street Sound: *Up the Yard with Jamsy* (Kay-Tel).

The Bushy Park Rangers: *Come Out of Those Bushes And Take It Like a Man* (Bottom Records).

Lou Kelly and the Swinging Beards: *Drink 'til You Puke, Boys!* (Ancient).

All the above titles are available through the author's own mail-order service, Dublin to Your Door.

CONCLUSION

If you've managed to reach this point without dozing off or consulting your legal people, then it's fair to presume that you are now approximately eighty per cent TRUE BLUE REAL DUB. As such your ability to entertain, enlighten and edify will soon be legendary. Before long you will be sidling up to strangers in bars and regaling them with yarns, little-known facts, snippets of poetry and snatches of old walking songs. The following final section will positively guarantee that you achieve this end. It contains the most comprehensive lexicon of Dublinese ever compiled and will, I am sure, prove an invaluable companion as you talk your way through the streets broad and narrow. Always treat it with respect – many hours of painstaking research and many hangovers have been endured in attempting to take Dublin's Mother

Tongue out of the oral domain and into the world of letters.

The mellifluous phrases herein should not so much trip off the tongue as stagger sideways out of the mouth. Memorise as many as possible and you will be astonished at the speed with which you 'blend in'. Soon you could be driving your own bus or unblocking Southsiders' pipes or abusing culchies from the Hill. Soon you could be thwarting and tormenting those hateful New Irelanders with your cunning linguistics.

The world is your mixed metaphor, as the man said. So remember: If you can't lick 'em, Mother Tongue them instead.

Slán abhaile.

DK

GLOSSARY OF REAL DUB TERMINOLOGY

(Including multifarious interjections and ejaculations)

GENERAL

How's it goin'/cutting. *Also:* **Howayah**: Hello (informal).

Take it handy/Good luck/See yeh: Goodbye.

Gimme: Please (can I have).

Tanks/Dat's grand: Thank you.

You're all right: You are welcome.

How's tricks/Every little ting?:How are you?

Dare's no point complaining: I am well.

Give us a go of dat: May I help/be of assistance?

Fire away!:Go right ahead.

Gerrouda me way, ye bollix: Excuse me.

I'm going to beat you up: I demand satisfaction.

I'll knock de bollix off yeh: You're claimed.

Hould your horses!: Stop!

Grand/I will in me arse/Dat would be tellin': Yes/No/Maybe.

Whaddya askin' *me* for?: I don't know.

As if *I* know: I have no idea.

Wha'?: Could you repeat that?

Dat's gobbledeegook: What does this mean?

I'm witcha: I understand [I am with you].

Are yeh with me?: Do you understand?

What in de name of Jaysus are yeh saying to me?: Could you say that in Dublinese.

D'you lads know anny English?: Is there someone here who speaks English?.

Can ye give us a dig out?: Could you help me?.

Dat's gift!: Fantastic.

What's dat yoke called?: What do you call this in Dublinese?.

I broke me hole laughing: That was most amusing.

Dis/Dat/Dese/Dose: This/That/These/Those.

Who's yer man?: What's his name?

What's dat all about?: Why?

Pint/Half pint: More/Less.

SALUTIONS

How's she cutting?: Hello (familiar).

Dare yar now, Heh Heh: Hello (cautious)

How's it going dare, Head: "Meeting you has made my day, would you care to join me for a drink?" Also "Hello".

Ah, me ould brown son: A pre-multi-racial Dublin salutation. Means: "Greetings my old comrade, is it really that long since last we parlayed?"

Well if it isn't de bould Paddy/Mick/Seamus!: "Oh no, not you again."

ASKING DIRECTIONS

Is dare a pub/Michael Guiney's/chip shop around here? Where's the nearest bar/bargain superstore/fine restaurant, please?

COMMON TERMS

A Moxy Lot Of: Plenty.

A Grush: A stampede.

As The Man Said: Preamble to some insightful comment. "As the man said, 'you can take dem out of de bog, but you can't take de bog out of dem'."

Ball Of Malt: Glass of whiskey.

Bender: See 'steamer'.

Boxing The Fox: Stealing apples from orchards.

Brill!: Super! "Dat's brill!"

Chancer: Person of dubious ability. From "he chances his arm".

Chiseller: An infant or young child.

Cowboy: A fly-by-night tradesman.

Da: Father.

Deed And I Do: Indeed, that is correct.

Dozy: Stupid, e.g. "You're a dozy bollix."

Erncha? Aren't you? "You're goin down to dat bleedin' pub again, erncha?"

Four-By-Four: Vehicle seen mainly parked outside the Queens of Dalkey, not to be confused with two-be-four.

Game ball: That will do nicely.

Ganky: Filthy.

Geebag: Derived from the gaelic '*gaoth* (wind) bag (bag)'. Normally applies only to the fairer sex. "You talk too much" = "you're a bit of an ould geebag, missus". Means 'windbag'. Honest.

Go on ye good ting: Well done, that man.

Gobdaw/Shite: A witless person prone to saying stupid things.

Gouger: A pugnacious type.

Grand job: "That's excellent."

Grot: Woman of stomach-turning ugliness.

Gurrier: A fighter.

Hard chaw: Tough guy.

Head: Hard man

Head lar: The boss

Heart of the rowl: Taken from the traditional song 'Dicey Riley' — "oh de heart of de rowl is Dicey Riley". No one has a bull's notion what this means and as such it can be dropped into almost any conversation without anyone batting an eyelid.

He's a panic: He is most amusing.

Hooley: Party

Howayah: A Southsider term for Northsiders ("She's a bit of a howayah") also a salutation ("Howayah, head!").

Jax: Toilet.

Knacker: A dirty fighter.

Langer: Male pudendum.

Looper: An insane person. "He's a bit of a looper wid de drink on him."

Ma: Mother.

Morto: An expression of embarrassment derived from the word 'mortified'. "I was only morto when me ma walked in on me."

Mowldy: Old and dirty. "She's a mowldy ould wagon." And "His langer was only mowldy."

On the scratch: Drawing the dole.

One and one: Fish and chips.

Ould fellah/wan: Husband/wife.

Pint of plain: A pint glass of Guinness stout beer.

Scut: Naughty young boy. "C'mere yeh little scut 'til I clatter yeh."

Scutters: Diarrhoea.

Scuttered: Drunk.

Segosha: Term of endearment. "Ah, me ould segosha, dare y'are now."

Shaper: A rough individual.

Shortarse: A person of low stature.

Skanger: Ugly, and often desperate, man.

Skanky: Smelly.

Skite: Drinking session.

Slapper: A woman of low moral fibre.

Steamer: A person of alternative sexuality.

Swapping spits: Kissing.

The Job's Oxo: "Well that's that sorted out."

Thingummyjig: A yoke.

Tick: Thick, as in Stupid.

Two-Be-Four: A multi purpose piece of wood, 2" by 4" thick. Can be used in a variety of situations such as "A bit of two-be-four will fix dat missus", "Oh dat'd be de two-be-four missus, dare terrible tricky, at least £70 I'd say" and "C'mere 'til I smack you on de head wid dis two-be-four".

Wagon: A bossy woman.

Wha'?: Means "What?" but is used more as an aggressive demand for confirmation. "He's only a bolleeks wha'?". "It's a grand ould hooley, wha'?". "De arse on yer wummin, wha'?".

Whang: Smell. As in "De whang off your feet is only killin' me."

We're on de pig's back: Phrase normally associated with economic boom times akin to "Let the good times roll".

Yoke: A thingummyjig.

You can't beat a good big bowl of coddle: I am a liar, don't believe a word I say.

Young wan/lad: Girl/boy.

You're laughing: Go along now out of that.

MINOR AILMENTS

The Johnny Giles/Nobby Stiles: Haemorrhoids.

The Scutters: Diarrhoea

The Turkey Trots: As above.

The Runs: As above.

PUB PHRASES

I'm bleedin' locked: I am extremely drunk.

Out of me tree: I'm bleeding locked.

Threw me ring up: I have just reacquainted myself with my lunch.

Who opened dare lunch?: Did you just break wind?

Did ye ged off wid a young wan/fellah?: Did you meet anyone nice last night?

Did ye drop de lawv?: Did you wake up with dirty fingernails and/or a tired wrist?

A slippier: A pint on the sly ("Cover for me while I go for a slippier")

Battle Cruiser: Boozer (as in pub).

A late one: After hours pint, more often than not a late six or seven. "I am just nipping down de Battle Cruiser for a late one, my love."

Locked: The mental state attained after going for a late one.

Locked out: The physical state attained after going for a late one.

Caught short: An unpleasant "accident" that can occur after getting locked after going for a late one (see 'Touch cloth').

Touch cloth: See 'Caught short'.

D'you know who owns dis pint?: I'm having this.

I do love de odd pint: Every third, fifth and seventh.

Your shout: It's your round.

It's not my shout: It is not my round.

Dat hit de spot: Delicious!
Your only man: That's a grand pint.

FOOD

Lyons Tea: Blend of tea formerly with black-faced minstrels as its brand logo.
Sliced pan: Bread.
Coddle: Milky stew of pigmeat and spuds.
Rashers: Slices of bacon.
Tripe: Sheep's stomach.
Boxty: Potato Cake.
Griddle cake: Similar to above.
A decent fry: Consists of sausages, rashers, black pudding, white pudding, fried eggs, fried bread, beans, tea and toast. And a heart monitor.

PHRASES USED IN DISCUSSIONS AMONGST FRIENDS:

Be de hokey: Well I never.
Gwan ourra dat: Go away out of that/really?
Me ould segosha: My very good friend.
Janey mac: Well I'll be blown.
C'mere 'til I tell yeh: Let me inform you.
Goway!: Are you kidding me?
Dyeknowwharrimean?: Am I making myself clear?

Juknowwharrimsayintyeh?: Do you know what
 I'm saying?

Sound as a pound: I concur.

Coolah Boolah: I concur with enthusiasm.

Fair play to yeh: Well met, my good man!

A decent ould skin: A person of exceptional virtue.

You're like a dog with two mickeys: You look
 pleased about something.

Gerroura dat garden: "Go on!" An exhortation
 akin to the culchie "Hup ye boy ye!"

I've a terrible goo on me: "I am very thirsty, would
 you care to join me for a pint?"

ARGUMENTS/ROWS

Wharrare youse bleedin' looking ah?: Would you
 care to fight me?

Leg it!: I don't wish to fight you.

I'll give you such a root up de hole: I do wish to
 fight you.

Geddup de yard: Shut up, you big liar.

C'mere 'til I burst you: You've got my dander up
 now.

Alls I said was …: Please don't burst me.

I'll get me big brudder after yeh: Leave me alone.

Ho Ho, it'll end in tears: Stop larking about.

Go and bite de butt end of me nut brown bollix:
 No, I won't stop larking about.

Stick it up yer swiss: Indulge in some rectal penetration (swiss = swiss roll = hole).

Relax de head: Steady on, now.

Who's asking? I don't care for your attitude.

You're wrecking me head: Desist, you are irritating me.

CURSES/INSULTS

- "May de hairs on your arse turn to drumsticks and beat de bollix off you."
- "You've a face like a well-slapped arse."
- "You look like a bulldog chewing a wasp."
- "If my dog looked like you, I'd paint a face on its arse and teach it to walk backwards."
- "If I had a garden full of mickeys, I wouldn't let you look over de wall."

TIME/OCCASIONS

When's last orders?: What time is it?

Dis minnit: Now [this minute]. As in "gis a pint dis minnit or I'll batter yeh."

It's on de way: Right away.

It's on de way: Soon.

It's on de way: Later.

Holliers: Holidays.

De Crimbo: Christmas.

What d'ye get me?: It's my birthday.

LOVE

I tink you're only bleedin' massive: I am attracted to you.

I wouldn't mind dropping de lawv[*] on your pal: Your friend is very attractive.

My buddy says he'd eat chips out of your knickers: My friend fancies you.

Gwan ourra dat, ye grot: You're not really my type.

De head on yer man/wummin: He/She is not very good-looking.

Wearing de face off/Getting off with: Kissing. E.g.: "I wore de face off her" and "I got off wid a real skanger last night."

I'll get me mot/fellah after you: I have a girlfriend/boyfriend.

Your mot's deadly, does she do de gee?: You're girlfriend is very beautiful, you must be a very happy man.

Of course I love you, amn't I riding you?: I love you, I swear.

Give us a frenchy: Kiss me now.

Get your hole: Make love. *Also* 'Get your whack'.

Mine's a pint: I only have safe sex. (See Real Dub Sex).

Get your own mot: Leave her alone, she's mine.

Do you do de gee?: Is it okay if I touch you there?

---

[*] From *Lámh*, Irish for Hand.

Dis is your last chance: I'm leaving tomorrow.

You dancing or wha'? *or* **Going for a bop, ye good ting?**: Would you care to dance?

I like pints *and* women: I'm bisexual.

AT THE BAR

Whaddya havin'?: [To male friends] May I buy you a drink?. [To strange women]: I'll swap you a pint for a quick ride.

Anny chance of an ould pint?: Would you buy me a drink?

I'm gee-eyed/rat-arsed/out of me tree/trollied: I am drunk.

You're locked!: Are you drunk?

All de best!!: Cheers!!

Pint of plain: Beer.

Hey Jem, I'm gumming for a pint: I'd like a beer.

A ball of malt: Glass of whiskey.

Are you lookin' for a smack in de gob?: I was here before you.

I am gay: I don't drink.

Anny strikers?: Do you have a light? (Strikers = matches.)

Jaysus, I feel a bit pukey: I feel like throwing up.

EATING OUT

Can we eat it here, it's raining outside?: Table for two, please.

Whaddya want?: Would you care to order?: *Or if there is a queue*: Next?.

Give us de...: I would like...

Smoked cod and chips: Chef's special.

Curry sauce (with a side order of chips): Sauce du jour.

Another smoked cod and chips: Poisson fumee au pomme sauté.

Ice cream (with chocolate chips): Dessert.

Hey, head!!: Waiter, waiter!!

Jaze, me mouth's as dry as a camel's hole: I need a jug of water.

What's dis ould shite?: I didn't order this.

Hey head, d'you charge extra for de fly?: Waiter, there's a fly in my curry sauce.

Dis sauce is so cold de fly has died of exposure: This curry sauce is cold. *Or on the Southside*: I didn't order *gazpacho,* my good man.

Dat's cat!: I don't like this.

Dat's bleedin' rapid!: I really like this/that's great.

What's de story with de cold curry sauce/burnt chips/etc.: I'd like to complain.

I'll sort you out, ye bollix: This is not the last you'll hear of this.

I'm only bursting for a slash: Where are the toilets?

Are you de head lar?: Are you the manager?

Gis a bottle of de Liebfraumilch: I'd like a bottle of wine.

We'll have it by the neck: There's no need to pour.